A

# MEMOIR

OF

# WILLIAM PENN.

Compiled by Allen C. Thomas

PHILADELPHIA:
PUBLISHED BY THE
ASSOCIATION OF FRIENDS FOR THE DIFFUSION OF RELIGIOUS
AND USEFUL KNOWLEDGE,
No. 109 NORTH TENTH STREET.
1874.

# NOTE.

This small volume has been carefully compiled, in order that a just view of the life and character of Wm. Penn may be readily accessible to the youthful reader, as well as to those of maturer age who cannot conveniently procure the larger volumes which contain in full his writings and his history. In it has been reprinted almost entire the publication of "The London Tract Association of Friends," entitled, "A BRIEF MEMOIR OF WILLIAM PENN," enlarged by copious selections from his letters, and particulars respecting his treaties with the Indian tribes. These have been taken mainly from Enoch Lewis' Life of William Penn, published in Vol. V. of "FRIENDS' LIBRARY," and from a publication entitled, "NORTH AMERICAN INDIANS AND FRIENDS," issued by the Aborigines' Committee of the London Meeting for Sufferings. The chapter respecting the calumnies of T. B. Macaulay has been prepared for this work from reliable and uncontroverted authorities.

# MEMOIR

OF

# WILLIAM PENN,

THE FOUNDER OF PENNSYLVANIA.

## CHAPTER I. 1644–1668.

HIS FATHER SIR WILLIAM PENN — WILLIAM PENN'S EDUCATION, DIVINE VISITATIONS, EXPULSION FROM OXFORD — DISPLEASURE OF HIS FATHER—INCIDENT AT PARIS — IMPRISONMENT IN IRELAND—BECOMES A FRIEND, AND REMAINS FIRM, THROUGH HIS FATHER'S OPPOSITION.

WILLIAM PENN was born in London in the year 1644. His father, Sir William Penn, was of an ancient family of Buckinghamshire, and became distinguished as a naval commander under the Commonwealth. Being attached however to the royal cause, he opened a correspondence with Charles, for which he was arrested and sent to prison; and, though soon pardoned and set at liberty, he at length united with Monk and others in bringing Charles to the throne. For this and other services he was in favour with the king and handsomely rewarded; and being a vain ambitious man, he was anxious to prepare his son for a brilliant worldly career. William however had a natural seriousness and independence of mind, which indisposed him to second his father's designs, and formed the basis of his manly christian character in after life.

When about twelve years old, and at school at Chigwell in Essex, he had a remarkable vision, or "visitation of heavenly light," which convinced him of the existence of a God, and of the capacity of the human soul to hold communion with Him. His mind was contrited under a sense of Divine love; and he believed himself called to a holy religious life. On entering the university of Oxford, his associations and pursuits tended to weaken these impressions: he studied hard, joined his fellow students in various sports, and became a general favorite. But the Lord preserved him in the midst of prevailing darkness and sin. He had a taste and ready capacity for learning, especially in the languages, history, and theology; entered with zest into puritanical discussions, and united with others in opposing the popish innovations encouraged by the Court. It was at this juncture that he first became acquainted with the religious views of the Friends, through the preaching of Thomas Loe, a minister of the Society, who held a meeting at Oxford. Young Penn and other students attended it, and being impressed with the doctrines declared, and with the simplicity and purity of true Christianity in opposition to a pompous, ceremonious ritual, they withdrew from the public services, and held meetings among themselves for divine worship in a more simple way. This attracted the notice of the superiors; the young nonconformists became the subject of obloquy and persecution, and were brought up, reprimanded, and fined; yet nothing daunted, they persevered in their course, and were soon afterwards on this account expelled from the college.

Sir William Penn was surprised and mortified at the conduct of his son, who, he had hoped, would be prepared to take a lead in fashionable and courtly circles; and, acting on the impulse of his feelings, he had recourse to threats and even the whip, and, after fruitless attempts to effect a change, turned him out of doors. This was in 1662. But the admiral, though violent in his temper, soon began to relent, and, being prevailed on by the intercessions of his wife, he resolved to try a gentle course, in the hope to be more successful. The gay scenes and manners of Paris might, he thought, banish the increasing gravity of his son, and as some persons of rank, whom he knew, were going to France on their travels, it was arranged that young Penn should accompany them. He remained some time at Paris, where, being presented to Louis XIV., he is said to have been a frequent guest at court. Such scenes, and an acquaintance with distinguished young men in the higher circles, effaced some of his former sedateness.

Here he met with an incident which he has recorded, for the purpose of showing the folly of those outward demonstrations of honour, which the pride

1*

of man has led him to invent and afterwards covet "What envy, quarrels and mischief," says he, in a work written after he became a Friend, "have happened among private persons, upon their conceit that they have not been respected according to their degree of quality among men, with hat, knee or title —even duels and murders not a few." In France I was myself once set upon, about eleven o'clock at night, as I was walking to my lodgings, by a person who waylaid me with his naked sword in his hand, and demanded satisfaction of me for taking no notice of him, at a time when he civilly saluted me with his hat, though, the truth was, I saw him not when he did it. Suppose he had killed me, for he made several passes at me, or that I in my defence had killed him, when I disarmed him; I ask any man of understanding or conscience, if the whole round of ceremony were worth the life of a man, considering the dignity of his nature and the importance of his life, with respect to God his Creator, himself, and the benefit of civil society. In the issue of this attack he displayed his humanity and regard for the life of a fellow-being, in permitting his assailant to pass away unharmed, though he had disarmed him, and had him completely in his power. At Saúmur he pursued his studies under Moses Amyrault, a learned protestant minister of Calvinistic principles. With him he read the works of early christian writers, paid attention to various branches of theology, and acquired a good knowledge of French literature. He then proceeded to the South of Europe, and having reached Turin, was suddenly recalled home by the admiral, in 1664, to take charge of the family affairs, during his own absence at sea.

The polished manners of young Penn, on his return to England, attracted much notice and gave his father great satisfaction, since they procured him access to the highest circles of society, and afforded hope of his obtaining that honour, which his fond parent so highly valued. With this view, he was entered as a student at Lincoln's Inn, that he might become acquainted with the laws of his country, and qualify himself for a public character. The great plague in London put an end to these studies; the awfulness of the visitation, and the sudden summons of death to thousands, aroused him, excited afresh his serious thoughtfulness, and parental hopes were again threatened with disappointment. In order to counteract this returning gravity, and at the same time to turn his stability to good account, Sir W. Penn now sent his son to Ireland to superintend his property, giving him letters of introduction to his friend the Duke of Ormond, who was then the Lord Lieutenant. At the Vice-regal Court he became very popular; and an insurrection having broken out at Carrickfergus, he volunteered to accompany Lord Arran, the Duke's son, who was sent to quell it. Distinguishing himself by great courage and coolness, he was invited to join the army as a profession — a proposal to which, with all the ardour and fickleness of youth, he was disposed to accede; but his father, happily for him and for the world, positively refusing his assent,

William reluctantly yielded, and retired to take charge of his father's estate at Shangarry, having also a government appointment at Kinsale.

But Divine Providence again interposed to change the current of his life, and to call him to that sphere in which he became so eminent. Being at Cork on business, he heard that Thomas Loe, whose preaching had interested him at Oxford, was to hold a religious meeting in the city that evening. Curiosity, and perhaps a higher motive, prompted him to stay and attend it, and deep was the impression which he received. After a time of silence, Thomas Loe rose with the words, "There is a faith that overcomes the world, and there is a faith that is overcome by the world." On this theme, which was peculiarly adapted to W. Penn's case, the preacher enlarged, carrying conviction to his mind, which had long oscillated between love to God on the one hand, and love to his father and to the world on the other. The conflicts of such a soul were feelingly described, and the path of duty was clearly pointed out. He could not resist the appeal, his sensations were deep and earnest, and from that time he regularly attended the meetings of Friends. His own description of his case, from early life down to this period, was thus afterwards given to some pious persons in Germany. "Here I let them know how and when the Lord first appeared to me, which was about the twelfth year of my age; how, at times, betwixt that and the fifteenth, he visited me, and the divine impressions he gave me of himself; of my persecution at Oxford, and how he sustained me in the midst of darkness and debauchery; of my being banished the college, the bitter usage I underwent when I returned to my father; of the Lord's dealings with me in France, and at the time of the great plague in London; the deep sense he gave me of the vanity of this world, and of the irreligiousness of the religions of it. Then, of my mournful and bitter cries to him, that he would show me his own way of life and salvation, and my resolutions to follow him, whatever reproaches or sufferings should attend me, and that with great reverence and brokenness of spirit. How, after all this, the glory of the world overtook me, and I was even ready to give myself up to it; seeing as yet no such thing as the primitive spirit and church on the earth. It was at this time that the Lord visited me with a certain sound and testimony of his eternal word, through one of those the world calls Quakers, namely Thomas Loe. I related the bitter mockings and scornings that fell upon me, the displeasure of my parents, the invectives and cruelty of the priests, the strangeness of all my companions, what a sign and wonder they made of me; but, above all, that great cross of watching against and resisting my own vain affections and thoughts."

The members of the Society of Friends were at that time severely persecuted, especially in Ireland. Their meetings for divine worship were often interrupted by the mob, and sometimes broken up by magistrates or soldiers; so that W. Penn had no reason to expect that he should escape. At a meeting held at Cork, he was apprehended with many besides, on the plea of a proclamation against tumultuous assemblies, and taken before the mayor; but that officer, observing his dress and general appearance to be different from those of the others, offered him liberty on his giving bond for his good behaviour — which refusing to do, he was with eighteen more committed to prison. While there, he addressed a manly appropriate letter to the Earl of Orrery, then President of Munster; declaring that he had committed no crime, and appealing to the Earl's clemency and sense of justice to grant him a discharge. In this letter may be seen the germ of that noble principle of liberty of conscience, which, through his remaining years, often and under much suffering, he boldly maintained; and which he was at length permitted to see generally recognized. The Earl at once ordered his release.

This imprisonment, far from cooling his zeal, deepened his sympathy with his new and suffering friends. He felt that a great principle was at stake, and he was freely willing to bear the reproaches and trials which in that age so largely befell them. The report that he had become a "Quaker" soon reached the Vice-regal Court, and also his father, who promptly ordered him home. At first the admiral perceived nothing peculiar in his dress or manners; but his seriousness increasing, and the usual ceremony of taking off the hat being omitted, he became dissatisfied and demanded an explanation. The interview was deeply touching and painful to both parties.

The son avowed his religious principles, and declared that as a duty to God he could not renounce them, at the same time assuring his father of his strong affection, of his respect, and of his sincere desire to obey him in every thing that did not conflict with his own christian duty. The father, on the other hand, expecting a peerage for himself, and having set his mind on advancing his son to wealth and honour, could not bear to see him forego the dazzling prize, and unite with the despised Quakers; which seemed to him little less than madness, and likely to bring contempt on the whole family. He not only reasoned with him, but condescended to entreat and implore him. The son, who tenderly loved his father, was deeply afflicted, but stood firmly to his principles. Finding that he could not prevail, the admiral desired him once more to uncover his head, at least, in the presence of the King, the Duke of York, and himself — a request which he promised to consider. Trivial and even proper, as this concession may appear to some, to William Penn it was no trifle. He retired to his chamber, and with fasting and prayer sought for divine guidance.

It was at that time customary to wear the hat in the house, even at meals, and to uncover the head was a mark of especial reverence. The same homage was paid to the Divine Being himself. The early Friends felt that all their actions, as well as their words, must be sincere and truthful, and that this principle of conduct was entirely opposed to the shallow politeness and false flattery of the world.

Knowing that all men have immortal souls, to be saved or lost, that Jesus Christ died equally for all, and that his Holy Spirit visits each one, without distinction of high or low, rich or poor, they felt that all men are essentially equal, from the king on his throne to the peasant in his cabin; and that the adventitious circumstances of prosperity or adversity are as nothing, in the scale of true merit and honour, which depend on obedience or disobedience to the law of God. They asserted the native dignity and equality of every man; and, while anxious to pay honour and respect where really due, they felt that these did not consist in the complimentary uncovering of the head, or the insincere use of deferential terms, but in plain, true, becoming language, and in civil, respectful behaviour. This view of the Christian's duty in conducting the intercourse of life formed part of their testimony to that simplicity, plainness, and truth, which they believed Christianity requires. "How can ye believe," said our Lord, "who receive honour one of another, and seek not the honour that cometh from God? Be not ye called Rabbi, for one is your master, even Christ, and all ye are brethren."

William Penn felt strongly the crisis to which he was brought; he was now in his twenty-fourth year; it seemed like the turning point of his life: this was only one matter out of many; and its concession would probably lead to further demands; hence his earnest supplication to be favoured with divine direction; that, without regard to worldly considerations, he might neither yield to unfounded objections on the one hand, nor compromise Christian principle on the other. The result was that he could feel no satisfaction, but in resolving to pursue the course he had entered on. At the next interview, therefore, he respectfully informed his father that he could not yield to the request. The admiral was no longer able to restrain his anger; he had tried every expedient; all his bright hopes for his son were dashed to the ground by his firmness, and he again indignantly expelled him from the house.

This was a time of extremity to the young convert. Brought up in affluence and dignity, caressed by the highest circles in the land, with the path to worldly greatness open before him, he had turned his back on them all, and incurred both penury and scorn for the sake of his religious principles. But, like Moses of old, he esteemed the reproach of Christ greater riches than the treasures of Egypt. He endured the cross with patience and magnanimity, and had peace within, which sustained him in firm hope and confidence. Some of his friends assisted him, his tender-hearted mother sent him money occasionally, and at length his father relented, though he did not openly countenance him.

## CHAPTER II. 1668–1670.

BECOMES A MINISTER AND AUTHOR — DISCUSSION WITH VINCENT — WRITES "SANDY FOUNDATION SHAKEN" — COMMITTED TO THE TOWER — WRITES "NO CROSS, NO CROWN," AND "INNOCENCY WITH HER OPEN FACE" — DISCHARGED AFTER EIGHT MONTHS AND A HALF.

THE Society of Friends, or Quakers, had now existed for nearly twenty years, through a period of much conflict and severe persecution, which still continued. Its Christian doctrines were clearly ascertained, and laid before the public; a wholesome system of church discipline was established. The accession of a conscientious, well educated, and talented young man, like William Penn, was of great value to it. He became a member from deep conviction, and by degrees laid aside his sword, his ornaments, and his gay attire.

Whilst thus approaching that purer standard of Christian principle, which soon afterward he openly upheld and suffered for, it is related that he met with George Fox, and asked his advice respecting the wearing of his sword, as he might appear singular among Friends in consequence; and that George Fox replied, "I advise thee to wear it as long as thou canst." Not long after they met again, when William Penn had no sword, and George Fox said to him, "William, where is thy sword?" "Oh," said he, "I have taken thy advice, I wore it as long as I could."

The earnest conviction which thus led to the entire abandonment of the vain fashions of the world, drew him soon after, to write to a young acquaintance, who was captivated by them. In this letter, he says, "And canst thou imagine that those holy men recorded in Scripture, spent their days, as do the gallants of these times? Where is the self-denying life of Jesus, the cross, the reproach, the persecution, and loss of all, which He and His suffered, and most willingly supported, having their eyes fixed upon a more enduring substance. Well, my friend, this know, and by these shalt thou be judged, and in it I am clear, That as without holiness none can see God, so without subjection to that Spirit, Light, or Grace in the heart, which God in love hath made to appear to all, that teacheth to deny all ungodliness and worldly lusts, and to live soberly, righteously, and godly in this present world; I say without subjection hereunto, there is no attaining to that holiness which will give thee an entrance into His presence, in which is joy and pleasure for ever. Examine thyself, how remote thou art from the guidings and instructions of this Spirit of Grace, who canst countenance this age in frequenting their wicked and vain sports, plays and entertainments, conforming thyself to ridiculous customs, and making one at idle talking and vain jesting, wheresoever thou comest, not considering thou shalt account to God for every idle word. And let all thy frolicking associates know, the day is hastening, in which they shall not abide the presence of Him that sits upon the throne. It shall be a time of horror, amazement and distress. Then shall they know there is a righteous, holy Judge of all. As for thee, with pity is thy condition often in my thoughts, and often is it my desire that thou mayst do well; but whilst I see thee in that spirit, which savours of this world's delights, ease, plenty and esteem, neglecting that one thing necessary, I have but little hopes. However, I could not let this plain admonition pass me; and what place soever it may have in thy thoughts, I am sure it is in true love to that which shall be happy or miserable to all eternity. I have not sought fine words or chiming expressions; the gravity, the concernment and nature of my subject, admit no such butterflies. In short, be advised, my friend, to be serious, and to ponder that which belongs to thy eternal peace. Retire from the noise and clatter of tempting visibles, to the beholding Him who is invisible, that He may reign in thy soul, God over all, exalted and blessed for ever. Farewell.

I am thy well-wishing, real friend,

William Penn."

In 1668, a few months after his expulsion from the parental home, he came forward, from an apprehension of religious duty, in the important character of a minister of the gospel. His qualifications both natural and spiritual for this service were of a high order. Both in word and writing, he was terse in expression, rich in instruction, original and uncompromising in sentiment. He became eminent as a minister and an author, and was thus described by one of his friends, "Sent of God to teach others what himself had learned, he was rightly called and qualified for the work: commissioned from on high to preach to others that holy self-denial himself had practised; to recommend to all that serenity and peace of mind himself had felt; walking in the light, to call others out of darkness; having drunk of the water of life, to direct others to the same fountain; having tasted of the heavenly bread, to invite all men to partake of the same banquet; being redeemed by the power of Christ, he was sent to call others from under the dominion of Satan into the glorious liberty of the sons of God, that they might receive remission of sins, and an inheritance among them that are sanctified, through faith in Jesus Christ. One workman thus qualified," says the same author, "is able to do his Master's business far more effectually than ten bold intruders, who undertake to teach a science themselves never learned."

Many of William Penn's publications were controversial, and, in consistence with the character of the age, contained strong, severe, and sometimes unguarded expressions; they were therefore more adapted to that period than to later times. As an independent and a comprehensive thinker, a firm champion of religious liberty, breathing forth generous, manly, and noble sentiments, chastened by love to God and man, most of his writings will stand the test of inquiry, and several of them cannot fail to be valued so long as that which is truly excellent shall be appreciated. His early compositions were penned with the lively zeal of a new convert. The first bears the title of "Truth exalted," and in energetic terms calls upon princes, priests, and people, to examine the grounds of their faith, and to compare them with the true Christian standard. His acts corresponded with his writings. Going down to Whitehall with a few of his friends, he obtained an audience of the Duke of Buckingham, and pressed on him the necessity of toleration for dissenters, pleading their right to far better treatment than the indignities they then suffered, appealing to the old laws of England, to ancient customs and charters. Nor were his reasonings in vain: the duke promised to bring a Bill into Parliament to redress the evils complained of, but, though he kept his word, the Commons rejected the measure.

A circumstance now occurred, which led to consequences both important and painful. There lived in Spitalfields a Presbyterian minister named Thomas Vincent, two of whose hearers being convinced of the doctrines held by Friends, forsook their former pastor. This exciting his animosity, he traduced the Quakers in violent terms, pronouncing their doctrines erroneous and damnable, and William Penn a Jesuit. Hearing of these charges, William Penn and George Whitehead, an eminent minister of the Society, went to Vincent, and demanded a public opportunity to clear themselves. After some demur, Vincent appointed a time, but at his own meeting-house; and, to insure a majority, he called his congregation together at an earlier hour, and pre-occupied the place. When Penn and Whitehead arrived, they found Vincent declaiming against them, whereupon they required to be heard in their own defence; but Vincent proposed that he should question them, which was agreed to by the people, who were mostly his own followers. He then began to examine them as to their belief in the nature of the Divine Being, the Trinity, the doctrines of imputed righteousness and of satisfaction for sin, using gross and unscriptural terms. These being objected to by the Friends, and the language of Holy Scripture appealed to, he and his audience attempted to put them down with accusations of blasphemy and reproach; and, refusing them liberty to explain, he dismissed his people, extinguished the candles, and withdrew. Not deterred by this unfair treatment, they persisted in the dark to address those who remained, till Vincent came back and promised them another hearing; a promise which, however, he did not fulfil.

William Penn now resorted to the press to set forth his views on the points in question, and in the fervour of youthful zeal, against what he believed to be error on the one hand, he laid himself open to the imputation of error in the opposite direction. "The Sandy Foundation shaken," was the title of his essay: it gave great offence to the bishop of London and other theologians of the day, who pronounced it heretical. Penn was also anonymously accused of treasonable designs, and the government was prevailed on to issue an order for committing him to the Tower. Here his treatment was severe; he was immured in a solitary cell; nor was he permitted to see his family or friends, except now and then his father, who commiserated and visited him. The bishop evidently hoped to awe him into submission, but he little knew the character of his captive. One day Penn's servant brought him word that it was resolved he should either publicly recant, or die in prison. He only smiled at the menace, saying, "They are mistaken in me; I value not their threats; I will weary out their malice; my prison shall be my grave before I will budge a jot, for I owe my conscience to no mortal man."

Prepared patiently and firmly to endure all the sufferings that might await him, he now betook himself diligently to writing. His chief work had a title suited to his own feelings, and to the experience of every true Christian — "No Cross, no Crown." It consists of two parts. In the first, he reviews the corrupt state of Christendom, shows the necessity of daily bearing the cross of Christ, describes its practical nature, the duty of self-denial, the evils of pride, avarice, and luxury; dividing each into several branches, and pleading for simplicity, contentment, and a life of faith. In the second part, he quotes the testimonies of the greatest men of antiquity among the heathen; of Jesus Christ and his first disciples, and of early Christian writers, with the dying testimonies of many eminent moderns, in confirmation of the same views. In a preface to a later edition, he says, of the way of the cross, "It is a path, God in his everlasting kindness guided my feet into, in the flower of my youth, when about two and twenty years of age: then he took me by the hand, and led me out of the pleasures, vanities, and hopes of the world. I have tasted of Christ's judgments, and of his mercies, of the world's frowns and reproaches: I rejoice in my experience, and dedicate it, [reader,] to thy service in Christ. It is a debt I have long owed; I have now paid it, and delivered my soul. To my country, and to the world of Christians I leave it. May God, if he please, make it effectual to them all." The "No Cross, no Crown," was a remarkable work, especially considering the circumstances under which it was written. It would seem to have required a large library and great research, and produced an impression highly creditable to the writer. It went rapidly through several editions, and has often been reprinted in modern times.

From a chapter, entitled "The Serious Testimonies of Dying, as well as Living Men," we select the following examples:

The first from Bulstrode Whitlock, an associate of those great men whom the lords and commons of England appointed to treat with King Charles I. for peace. "He was commissioner of the great seal, and ambassador to Sweden, a scholar, a lawyer, a statesman; in short, he was one of the most accomplished men of the age. Being with him sometimes at his own house in Berkshire, where he gave me the account of Chancellor Oxenstiern, among many serious things he spoke, this was very observable."

"I have ever thought," said he, "there has been one true religion in the world; and that is the work of the Spirit of God in the hearts and souls of men. There have been, indeed, divers forms and shapes of things, through the many dispensations of God to men, answerable to his own wise ends, in reference to the low and uncertain state of man in the world; but the old world had the Spirit of God, for it strove with them; and the new world has had the Spirit of God, both Jew and Gentile, and it strives with all; and they that have been led by it, have been the good people in every dispensation of God to the world. And I, myself, must say, I have felt it from a child, to convince me of my evil and vanity; and it has often given me a true measure of this poor world, and some taste of divine things; and it is my grief, I did not more early apply my soul to it. For, I can say, since my retirement from the greatness and hurries of the world, I have felt something of the work and comfort of it, and that it is both ready and able to instruct, and lead, and preserve those who will humbly and sincerely hearken to it. So that my religion is the good Spirit of God in my heart; I mean what that has wrought in me and for me."

After a meeting at his house, to which he gave an entire liberty for all that pleased to come, he was so deeply affected with the testimony of the light, spirit, and grace of Christ in man, as the gospel dispensation, that after the meeting closed in prayer, he rose up, and pulled off his hat, and said, "This is the everlasting Gospel I have heard this day; and I humbly bless the name of God, that he has let me live to see this day, in which the ancient Gospel is again preached to them that dwell upon the earth."

"Count Oxenstiern, Chancellor of Sweden, was a person of the first quality, station, and ability in his own country, whose share and success, not only in the chief ministry of affairs in that kingdom, but in the greatest negotiations of Europe during his time, made him no less considerable abroad. After all his knowledge and honour, being visited in his retreat from public business, by Commissioner Whitlock, ambassador to Queen Christina, in the conclusion of their discourse, he said to the ambassador, 'I have seen much and enjoyed much of this world, but I never knew how to live till now. I thank my God that has given me time to know Him and to know myself. All the comfort I have, and all the comfort I take, and which is more than the whole world can give, is feeling the good Spirit of God in my heart, and reading in this good book, holding up the Bible, that came from it. You are now in the prime of your age and vigour, and in great favour and business; but this will all leave you, and you will one day better understand and relish what I say to you; and then you will find that there is more wisdom, truth, comfort and pleasure, in retiring and turning your heart from the world, to the good Spirit of

God, and in reading the Bible, than in all the favour of courts and princes. This I had, as near as I am able to remember, from the ambassador's own mouth more than once. A very edifying history when we consider from whom it came; one of the greatest and wisest men of his age; while his understanding was as sound and vigorous, as his experience and knowledge were great."

> "The specious inconveniences that wait
> Upon a life of business and of state,
> He sees, nor doth the sight disturb his rest."

"My own father, after thirty years' employment, with good success, in divers places of eminent trust and honour in his own country, upon a serious reflection not long before his death, spoke to me in this manner: 'Son William, I am weary of the world; I would not live my days over again if I could command them with a wish; for the snares of life are greater than the fears of death. This troubles me, that I have offended a gracious God, who has followed me to this day. O have a care of sin! That is the sting both of life and death. Three things I commend to you—First: Let nothing in this world tempt you to wrong your conscience; I charge you do nothing against your conscience; so will you keep peace at home, which will be a feast to you in the day of trouble. Secondly: Whatever you design to do, lay it justly, and time it seasonably, for that gives security and despatch. Lastly: Be not troubled at disappointments; for if they may be recovered do it; if they cannot, trouble is vain. If you could not have helped it be content; there is often peace and profit in submitting to Providence; for afflictions make wise. If you could have helped it, let not your trouble exceed instruction for another time. These rules will carry you with firmness and comfort through this inconstant world.'"

This excellent treatise is thus concluded: "Wherefore, since we are compassed about with so great a cloud of witnesses, let us lay aside every weight and burden, and the sin and vanities, which so easily beset us, and with a constant holy patience run our race, having our eyes fixed upon Jesus, the author and finisher of our faith, not minding what is behind; so shall we be delivered from every snare. No temptations shall gain us, no frowns shall scare us from Christ's cross and our blessed self-denial: and honour, glory, immortality, and a crown of eternal life, shall recompense all our sufferings in the end."

"Oh Lord God! thou lovest holiness, and purity is thy delight in the earth. Wherefore, I pray thee, make an end of sin and finish transgression, and bring in thy everlasting righteousness to the souls of men, that thy poor creation may be delivered from the bondage it groans under, and the earth enjoy her Sabbath again: That thy great name may be lifted up in all nations, and thy salvation be renowned to the ends of the world. For thine is the kingdom, the power and the glory, for ever. Amen."

By the King's command, Stillingfleet, bishop of Worcester, visited William Penn in prison, and reasoned candidly with him. After lying there six months, and seeing no prospect of a release, he wrote to Lord Arlington, the secretary of state, a manly forcible remonstrance against his detention, and the treatment he suffered. He declares his own belief in "the eternal deity of Christ," protests against punishments by the civil power for differences of religious opinion, asserts that the understanding can be moved only by reason, not by force, appeals to the King, and maintains his entire innocence of crime. Finding that his views on some of the points debated were much misunderstood, he stated them more fully and clearly to the public in a short but vigorous pamphlet, entitled "Innocency with her open Face; presented by way of apology for the Sandy Foundation shaken." In this piece, while he does not retract, he explains and vindicates, the soundness of his Christian faith.

He thus declares his belief, "I sincerely own and unfeignedly believe, by virtue of the sound knowledge and experience, received from the gift of that holy unction and Divine grace inspired from on high, in One holy, just, merciful, Almighty and Eternal God, who is the Father of all things; who appeared to the holy patriarchs and prophets of old at sundry times, and in divers manners; and in one Lord Jesus Christ, the everlasting Wisdom, Divine power, true Light, only Saviour and Preserver of all; the same One holy, just, merciful, Almighty and Eternal God, who, in the fulness of time, took and was manifested in the flesh. At which time He preached, and his disciples after him, the everlasting Gospel of repentance, and promise of remission of sins and eternal life, to all that heard and obeyed." And again, "Let all know this, that I pretend to know no other name, by which remission, atonement, and salvation, can be obtained, but Jesus Christ the Saviour, who is the wisdom and power of God."

Soon after it was issued, and probably at the instance of the Duke of York, he was set at liberty, after an imprisonment of eight months and sixteen days.

William Penn had now the satisfaction of once more visiting his friend Thomas Loe, whom the Lord had made instrumental to convince him. He was then on his dying bed, and thus addressed William Penn, "Dear heart, bear thy cross. Stand faithful for God, and bear thy testimony in thy day and generation, and God will give thee an eternal crown of glory that shall not be taken from thee. There is no other way that shall prosper, than that which the holy men of old have walked in. God hath brought immortality to light, and life immortal is felt. Glory, glory, for He is worthy. Glory be to His name for evermore. My heart is full, what shall I say? His love overcomes my heart, my cup runs over, my cup runs over. He is come, He has appeared, and will appear." To others, he said, "Friends, keep your testimony for God, live with Him, and He will live with you."

Admiral Penn had become involved in trial and difficulty through the jealousy of rival commanders, especially Monk and Rupert, and he was saved from ruin only by the personal regard of the King and his brother. These trials softened his feelings towards his son, and his wish was indirectly conveyed to William that he should again take charge of his estates in Ireland. This he was not slow to fulfil; and proceeding to Shangarry in the summer of 1669, he remained there for some months, maintaining a frequent correspondence with his father, and successfully exerting himself to relieve his friends from suffering. A sensible decline in his father's health at length caused his return to England; a full reconciliation took place, and he became a resident in the parental mansion.

## CHAPTER III. 1670.

THE CONVENTICLE ACT—MEMORABLE TRIAL OF W. PENN AND W. MEAD AT THE OLD BAILEY, WITH THEIR INTREPID DEFENCE.

In the year 1670, William Penn was again a sufferer on account of his religious principles, and though the imprisonment to which he was subjected did not exceed a month in duration, yet his resolute conduct on the trial, in opposition to the tyrannical proceedings of the civic authorities, tended greatly to confirm his reputation, as a defender of civil and religious freedom, and to establish on a more solid foundation the liberties of his countrymen.

The severe Act against conventicles, which had been passed six years before, was now on the point of expiring, and the public mind was much agitated on the question of its renewal. The desire of the bishops, together with general apprehensions of the secret designs of the Duke of York and the Catholics, operated strongly in its favour, and it was but feebly opposed by the now crushed spirit of constitutional freedom. Though the government wished to except Protestant dissenters from its operation, the ecclesiastics, who feared the Puritan as much as the Romish influence, would not consent. The Act was consequently passed, declaring it seditious and unlawful, for more than five persons in addition to one family to assemble together for divine worship, in any other way than according to the liturgy. Every person so assembling was to be fined five shillings for the first offence, and ten shillings for the second; the preacher to forfeit twenty pounds for the first, and forty pounds for the second offence; and the owner of the house twenty pounds. Any magistrate refusing to act herein to be fined one hundred pounds, and every constable five pounds. One third of the fines to go to the informer. The Act to be construed most largely for the suppression of conventicles, and for the encouragement of those employed in its execution. Any justice to hear, convict, and levy privately, in opposition to the great charter which directed trial by jury.

William Penn soon became an offender under this unrighteous law, and it was determined not to deal with the case privately, but to make him a public example. He and others, going to the meeting-house in Gracechurch Street one morning at the usual hour, found it closed, and the doors guarded by soldiers; which was the case that day with all dissenters' places of worship, throughout the city. After a time, a considerable company being collected, he took off his hat, and began to address them in the street; on which the constables arrested both him and William Mead, a Friend, who was one of the hearers, and brought them before the Lord Mayor, Sir Samuel Starling, who committed them to Newgate; making no secret of his malice against William Penn and his father, and of his pleasure at having this opportunity to vent it. A full account of the celebrated trial was afterwards drawn up by William Penn, and has been often republished; a few particulars only can be given here. Not thinking it right passively to submit to illegal treatment, as many of his friends had done, he boldly asserted the rights of Englishmen, and succeeded in vindicating them.

On the first of the seventh month, (then September) 1670, the two prisoners were brought to the bar of the Old Bailey for trial; and the jury being called over, the indictment was read, which charged the prisoners, that with force and arms, they and others had met together, unlawfully and tumultuously, to the great disturbance of the peace, and to the great terror of many of the people. To this they pleaded Not guilty in the manner and form stated; and after being kept waiting for five hours, the Court adjourned.

Two days after they were again brought into the Court, when, on one of the officers taking off their hats, the Lord Mayor sternly ordered him to put them on again, and the Recorder fined them forty marks each for contempt of the court in wearing them. Three witnesses were called, but failed to prove the more offensive part of the charge. William Penn then said, that he and his friend freely acknowledged the fact of their meeting together for the worship of God; that they believed it their duty to do so, and that all the powers on earth should not prevent them from it. Sheriff Brown exclaimed, that he was not there for worshipping God, but for breaking the law.

W. PENN. — "I have broken no law, nor am I guilty of the indictment. I desire to know on what law you prosecute me, and ground the indictment."

THE RECORDER. — "On the common law."

PENN. — "Where is that common law?"

RECORDER. — "You must not think that I can run up so many years, and over so many adjudged cases, which we call common law, to satisfy your curiosity."

PENN. — "If it be common, it should not be so very hard to produce."

RECORDER. — "Sir, will you plead to your indictment?"

PENN.—"Shall I plead to an indictment that has no foundation in law? If you decline to produce the law, the jury will not be able to bring in their verdict." This so exasperated the Recorder, that he said, "You are a saucy fellow: speak to the indictment."

PENN. — "It is my place to speak to matter of law. I am arraigned a prisoner; my liberty, which is next to life itself, is concerned; and unless you show me and the people the law you ground your indictment upon, I shall take it for granted your proceedings are merely arbitrary." Here several on the bench, being much annoyed, bore hard on the prisoner to put him down; but he, undismayed, retained his calm, yet firm behaviour, neither party referring to the late Conventicle Act.

RECORDER.—"The question is, whether you are guilty of this indictment."

PENN.—"No; the question is, whether this indictment be legal. It is an imperfect answer, to say it is common law, unless we know both where and what that is; for where there is no law there is no transgression, and that which is not in being, is so far from common, that it is no law at all."

RECORDER.—"You are an impertinent fellow. Will you teach the Court what law is? It is *lex non scripta*,—that which many have studied thirty or forty years to know; and would you have me tell you in a moment?"

PENN.—"If the common law be so hard to be understood, it is far from being common: but if the Lord Coke in his Institutes be of any consideration, he tells us that common law is common right, and that common right is the great charter privileges confirmed."

RECORDER.—"Sir, you are a troublesome fellow, and it is not for the honour of the Court to suffer you to go on."

PENN.—"I design no affront to the Court, but to be heard in my just plea; and I may plainly tell you that if you deny me the oyer of that law, which you say I have broken, you do at once deny me an acknowledged right, and evince to the world your resolution to sacrifice the privileges of Englishmen to your sinister and arbitrary designs."

The Court were extremely irritated at William Penn's spirited behaviour, and the more so because what he said was so just and reasonable that they could not answer him. Ashamed probably to shield themselves under the late Conventicle Act, they made no reference to it, but, in order to silence him, directed that he should be put into the bale-dock, while he loudly remonstrated against their arbitrary conduct.

William Mead, being now left alone, showed equal firmness, and thus addressed the jury: "I stand here to answer an indictment which is full of falsehoods, charging me with meeting with force and arms, unlawfully and tumultuously: whereas I dare not make use of arms, but am a peaceable man, and therefore William Penn's question was a very proper one. You men of the jury, if the Recorder will not tell you what makes a riot or an unlawful assembly, Coke tells us that a riot is when three or more are met together to beat a man, enter forcibly into his land," &c. The Recorder then scornfully pulled off his hat, and said, "I thank you, sir, that you will tell me what the law is." To which W. Mead replied, "Thou mayest put on thy hat, I have never a fee for thee now."

MAYOR.—"You deserve to have your tongue cut out."

MEAD.—"Thou didst promise me that I should have fair liberty to be heard. Why may I not have the privileges of an Englishman?"

He too was now ordered into the bale-dock, and in their absence the Court charged the jury, contrary to law and precedent; against which William Penn protested from a distance. The prisoners were then removed to a loathsome cell in Newgate.

After an absence of two hours, the jury returned, the prisoners were sent for, and a verdict was delivered against William Penn, "Guilty of speaking in Gracechurch Street." The Court, dissatisfied with this verdict, told the jury they might as well have said nothing; and after threats, and attempting in vain to extort something more, sent them out again. In half an hour they returned, bringing a written verdict signed by them all, that they found William Penn guilty of speaking or preaching to an assembly in Gracechurch Street, and William Mead not guilty. This so provoked the Recorder, that he said to the jury, "Gentlemen, you shall not be dismissed till we have a verdict the Court can accept, and you shall be locked up without meat, drink, fire, or tobacco. We will have a verdict, or you shall starve for it."

PENN.—"My jury, who are my judges, ought not to be thus menaced: their verdict should be free and not compelled. I desire that justice may be done me." The Court being about to send back the jury, William Penn said, "The agreement of twelve men is a verdict in law, and such a one having been given, I require the clerk of the peace to record it at his peril." To the jury he said, "You are Englishmen; mind your privileges, give not away your rights." To which some of them replied that they never would.

The trial having excited general interest, the Court had been thronged throughout, and was now adjourned till nine the next morning: when the jury, being called, brought in the same verdict as before. The magistrates were more exasperated than ever, and behaved towards them in a most unbecoming and unconstitutional manner, refusing to accept their verdict of Not guilty for William Mead. William Penn again remonstrated in plain and pointed language, but to no good effect, the Court obstinately pursuing its arbitrary course, and the Mayor crying out, "Stop his mouth, jailor; bring fetters and stake him to the ground." To this William Penn answered, "Do your pleasure: I matter not your fetters." The Recorder then acknowledged, "Till now I never knew the policy of the Spaniards, in suffering the Inquisition. It will never be well with us till something like it be brought into England." The jury, though very unwilling, were sent back, and kept through another night, without food or other accommodation. At seven the next morning, the prisoners were again placed at the bar in a crowded court, and the jury, who were much worn by long detention and fasting, returned each prisoner "Not guilty." This verdict gave general satisfaction to the people assembled, but was a great mortification to the Bench, who were compelled to accept it.

William Penn and William Mead now demanded their liberty, but were fined for alleged contempt of court, in not taking off their hats; and the jury, instead of being discharged, were fined forty marks each for their pretended obstinacy. Both parties were committed to Newgate for non-payment The imposition of fines on a jury was a daring attack on the rights of the subject, and was brought before the Court of Common Pleas by Edward Bushel, the most resolute of the jurors, when it was argued at length, and being pronounced altogether illegal, they were liberated. Admiral Penn, then on his death-bed, being anxious to see his son once more, is supposed to have paid the fines, and the two prisoners also were set at liberty. A late writer remarks, "The importance of this extraordinary trial can hardly be over-estimated, as a stand taken once for all upon the ancient liberties of England, against the encroachments of those in authority. It established a great truth — that unjust laws are powerless, when used against an upright people."

## CHAPTER IV. 1670–1677.

DYING ADVICE OF SIR WILLIAM PENN — W. P. TRAVELS AS A MINISTER — ACCOUNT OF GULIELMA MARIA SPRINGETT — AGAIN IMPRISONED IN THE TOWER — VISITS HOLLAND — MARRIES G. M. SPRINGETT — VISITS THE CONTINENT TWICE — RELIGIOUS CONVERSE WITH PRINCESS ELIZABETH — REPEATEDLY ADVOCATES TOLERATION.

ADMIRAL PENN lived but ten days after his son's release. Though he had not reached his fiftieth year, he had survived many changes, and experienced great trials. Many of his last remarks display a true knowledge of the world. "Son William," said he, "if you and your friends keep to your plain way of preaching, and to your plain way of living, you will make an end of the priests to the end of the world. Live in love, shun all manner of evil; I pray God to bless you, and he will bless you all." He left his son a good estate, producing an annual income of about fifteen hundred pounds; and sent messages to the King and the Duke of York, commending him to their kind offices; which they readily promised and endeavoured to fulfil.

William Penn now travelled as a minister of the gospel, holding considerable meetings, and preaching boldly the doctrines he professed. These doctrines, and especially that of the universality of Divine light or grace, being attacked by a Baptist minister named

Ives, in Buckinghamshire, he demanded an opportunity to vindicate them; and the parties met at Wycombe for discussion; but the assailant, as soon as he had stated his own arguments, unfairly withdrew. The people, however, more candid than their pastor, waited to hear the defence, which was satisfactory to most of them.

On visiting Oxford, William Penn found his friends there exposed to severe persecution for their religious principles, which struck at the root of the hierarchy; and as the Vice-Chancellor encouraged these proceedings, he addressed him in a letter of plain expostulation and reproof. Taking up his residence at the old family seat of Penn, in Buckinghamshire, he made the acquaintance of Gulielma Maria Springett, a very intelligent and interesting young person, then residing with her step-father, Isaac Pennington.

She was the daughter of Sir William and Mary Springett. Her father was a man of noble spirit, and conspicuous in the struggle for civil and religious liberty in England which resulted in the fall of Charles I., and the establishment of the Commonwealth. Whilst ardently engaged in this fearful contest, he was carried off by a fatal disease, resulting from the exposure incident to the inhuman practice of war. In 1642, a few weeks after his death, his daughter was born. Her mother, being deeply imbued with the love of Truth, became an earnest seeker after it, and withdrew from all participation in those worldly pleasures so inconsistent with it.

Several years afterwards, she met with Isaac Pennington, one, like herself, weary of the delights of this world, but seeking the haven of true rest. She says, "My love was drawn to him because I found he saw the deceit of all notions, and lay as one that refused to be comforted." After their marriage took place, they became members of the Society of Friends.

Residing at their estate of Chalfont, her daughter now approaching womanhood, the family were visited by Thomas Ellwood, who had in childhood been her playmate in familiar sports. His father and he were of the Cavalier sort, free and courtly in their manners, and, having known the Penningtons before their connection with Friends, were greatly surprised at the change in their demeanor, the seriousness of which kept down all light and airy conversation.

Thomas Ellwood, seeking the company of the daughter, says, "I found her gathering some flowers in the garden, attended by her maid, who was also a Quaker. But when I addressed myself to her, after my accustomed manner, with intent to engage her in some discourse which might introduce conversation on the foot of our former acquaintance, though she treated me with a courteous mein, yet, young as she was, the gravity of her look and behaviour struck such an awe upon me that I found myself not so much master of myself as to pursue any further conversation with her; whereupon, asking pardon for my boldness in having intruded myself into her private walks, I withdrew, not without some disorder of mind, at least as I thought"

Soon after this, Ellwood himself became a Friend,

and residing in this vicinity, was received in near intimacy with the Penningtons. It is stated that Gulielma was sought after by peers and commoners, courtiers and Puritans, being, as described by Ellwood, "a very desirable woman, whether regard was had to her outward person, which wanted nothing to render her comely, or to the endowments of her mind, which were every way extraordinary and highly obliging, or to her outward fortune, which was fair." "To all, in their respective turns, till he at length came for whom she was reserved, she carried herself with so much evenness of temper, such courteous freedom, guarded with the strictest modesty, that, as it gave encouragement or ground of hopes to none, so neither did it administer any matter of offence or just cause of complaint to any."

A pamphlet of the Roman Catholics falling in the way of William Penn, drew his close attention to their leading doctrines, and in a tract entitled "A Seasonable Caveat against Popery," he undertook to refute them, appealing to the authority of Scripture and of the early Christian Church, and clearly showing that his own views were entirely at variance with theirs. Notwithstanding this, he declared himself decidedly opposed to all persecution of Roman Catholics or others for their principles, and friendly to universal toleration.

His firm, intrepid conduct, both in asserting boldly, by word and writing, what he believed to be the truth, and in patiently suffering for it, with his earnest denunciations of all persecution and oppression, had rendered him obnoxious to those in authority, and they eagerly sought an opportunity to lay hold of him. Spies and informers, then so often employed, were set to watch and report his movements, and word being one day brought to Sir J. Robinson, that he was to be at a meeting at Wheeler Street the next morning, a sergeant and soldiers were sent to the place, and as soon as he stood up to preach, they pulled him down and delivered him to a constable, who conveyed him to the Tower. Here he was examined in the evening by several of those who had sat in judgment upon him only a few months before; Sir J. Robinson, pretending at first not to know him, then to feel great regard and pity for him, and afterwards accusing him with stirring up sedition, but when questioned, totally unable to prove it. In the course of the examination, Robinson again charged William Penn with being as bad as other folks, abroad and at home too; when he replied, "I make this bold challenge to all men, women, and children upon earth, justly to accuse me of ever having seen me drunk, heard me swear, utter a curse, or speak one obscene word,—much less that I ever made it my practice. Thy words shall be thy burden, and I trample thy slander under my feet." To another taunting remark of Robinson's, he replied, "I would have thee, and all other men to know, that I scorn that religion which is not worth suffering for, and able to sustain those that are afflicted for it; mine is, and whatever may be my lot for my constant profession of it, I am no ways careful, but resigned to answer the will of God by the loss of goods, liberty and life itself. When you have all, you can have no more; and then, perhaps, you will be contented, and by that you will be better informed of our innocency. Thy religion persecutes, mine forgives; and I desire my God to forgive you all that are concerned in my commitment, and I leave you all in perfect charity, wishing your everlasting salvation." The scene ended with their tendering him as before the oath of allegiance, which refusing to take, he was sent to Newgate again for six months. This was his second committal thither within four months; and Robinson even threatened to pull down the meeting-house; but the law placed it out of his power.

During this imprisonment, William Penn, as usual with him, was not idle. In a noisome, pestilential gaol, crowded with many of his friends, among felons and other criminals — a situation especially painful to a man of his refined feelings and habits, he produced several important treatises, chiefly in defence of liberty of conscience.

He and other prisoners also addressed, in a dignified and temperate style, the High Court of Parliament, which was then contemplating a more rigorous enforcement of the Act against conventicles, in opposition to a declaration of indulgence to tender consciences lately issued by the King, on his own authority.

The term of this imprisonment expiring, he resumed his religious labours in different parts;

extending them into Holland and Germany, where he met with many spiritually-minded persons.

Early in 1672, when in his twenty-eighth year, he married Gulielma Maria Springett, and settled at Rickmansworth in Hertfordshire, under circumstances of great comfort. Occasionally, he travelled as a minister, accompanied by his wife; and seldom was his pen without occupation, in vindicating the religious principles of the Society against assailants He also went to Whitehall to plead with the Court on behalf of George Fox, then a prisoner. Most of the principal religious men of that time were intolerant of others: William Penn, therefore, appeared in a novel character, by advocating both religion and toleration, which he did with much ability and force, in a treatise entitled "England's present interest considered."

Believing it his duty again to visit the continent, he proceeded in 1677 to Holland, in company with G. Fox, R. Barclay, and others; their object being to communicate "with many seeking persons," and to encourage them to more full dedication of heart to the Lord. They held religious meetings at Rotterdam, Haarlem, Amsterdam, &c., and organized a system of Church discipline for the small body of Friends in that country. In consequence of complaints which reached them of the sufferings of Friends of Dantzic, William Penn addressed a spirited letter on their behalf to John Sobieski, King of Poland, concluding with a saying of his predecessor Stephen, "I am king of men, not of consciences;

king of bodies, not of souls." In this letter, where he relates the most fundamental principles surely believed by Friends, we find this confession: "We do believe in the birth, life, doctrines, miracles, death, resurrection, and ascension of Jesus Christ our Lord; and that he laid down his life for the ungodly, not to continue so, but that they should deny their wickedness and ungodliness, and live soberly, righteously and godly in this present world, as the saints of old did, who were redeemed from the earth, and sat in heavenly places." Prosecuting their journey, they held interesting conferences and distributed tracts on religious subjects from place to place.

At Herwerden they visited the Princess Elizabeth, daughter of the King of Bohemia, and grand-daughter of James I., an illustrious and pious lady, with whom W. Penn had before corresponded. The visit, which was of a religious nature, proved to be a memorable one; the princess and her friend, the Countess De Hornes, receiving them with expressions of great kindness and openness.

Their first meeting having been held to satisfaction, a second interview with the family took place at the palace in the afternoon, and continued for five hours. "It was at this meeting" says W. Penn, "that the Lord in a more eminent manner began to appear. The eternal word showed itself a hammer that day — yea, sharper than a two-edged sword, dividing asunder between the soul and the spirit, the joints and the marrow. With hearts filled with holy thanksgivings to the Lord for his abundant mercy and goodness to us, we departed to our lodging." The next morning, at the suggestion of the Countess, a meeting was held for the inferior servants, at which "the same blessed power that had appeared, to visit them of high, visited them also of low degree." In the afternoon, the Princess and Countess reminded W. Penn of a promise he had made, to give them an account of his first convincement, and of the trials and consolations he had experienced in his religious course. After some pause he began his narrative, an extract from which has already been given, and which, being delivered with deep feeling, much affected the company, and was listened to throughout with earnest attention. The next afternoon another meeting for worship was held at the palace, several inhabitants of the town being invited; and the power of Divine Grace was again eminently manifested. At the close the Princess took William Penn by the hand, and endeavoured to express the sense she had of the presence and power of God, but could not proceed; and turning aside, she sobbed, saying, "I cannot speak to you, my heart is full."

At Cassel also "many received them tenderly and lovingly," among whom was one "Dureus, aged seventy-seven, who had forsaken his learning and school-divinity for the teachings of the Holy Spirit." Various other spiritual persons they met with in different classes of society, with whom they had serious intercourse; their concern being to call them to the substance and life of religion in the soul.

Meetings were held in other cities of Germany and were well attended. The Somerdykes, A. M. Schurman — a learned and pious lady, the Graef of Donau, a young Countess, and other seeking persons, were objects of their lively interest; and it seems to have been a time of great awakening in those parts. In this journey William Penn spent upwards of three months, and travelled nearly three thousand miles: it is the only portion of his religious labours of which he left a written narrative.

England was now disquieted with fears and pretended plots of the Roman Catholics: laws and oaths were made against them, and fell with severity on Friends, who declined to obey an unjust law, or to take an oath of any kind. William Penn twice attended Committees of the House of Commons, and represented the difficulties and cruelties under which his friends suffered; urging the duty of repealing all persecuting enactments on account of religion, where the public peace was not disturbed.

In written addresses to the government and the public, he repeatedly advocated the same great principles: which also induced him to use active exertions on two occasions to promote the return of his friend Algernon Sidney to Parliament. But the adverse influence of the Crown prevented his success.

## CHAPTER V. 1675–1685.

HIS CONNECTION WITH AMERICA — IS TRUSTEE FOR NEW JERSEY — OBTAINS A GRANT OF PENNSYLVANIA — ESTABLISHES FULL RELIGIOUS LIBERTY THERE — LETTER TO HIS WIFE AND CHILDREN—VISITS THE COLONY — TREATY WITH THE INDIANS — RETURNS AFTER TWO YEARS.

WILLIAM PENN must now be viewed in a new and very interesting character. From his early youth, he had been accustomed to hear from his father striking accounts of the other hemisphere. In his travels into Holland he had met with persecuted families, some of whose members had found peaceful shelter on American shores. Many English Puritans had sought refuge in the same wilderness land from harassing oppressors; and not a few of the Society of Friends, having followed their example, had already established general or yearly meetings on Rhode Island and in Maryland.

In 1675, he was called in as an arbitrator, to settle a difference between two of his friends, respecting a tract of land then called New Jersey, and he soon became a chief trustee and manager for the western part of that colony. Removing his own residence for the sake of greater retirement to Worminghurst in Surrey, he drew up a constitution for the infant colony, framed in the most liberal spirit. Commissioners and emigrants, most of whom were

Friends, went out, purchased the land of the Indians, and founded their little state on Christian principles. The part which he took in its affairs increased his strong interest in the new world, and made him long to found a refuge there, on a more extended scale, for the conscientious and persecuted.

When Admiral Penn died, he had large claims on the Government, chiefly for money lent, and these claims had increased in 1680, by the accumulation of interest, to upwards of £16,000. In consideration of this debt, the son petitioned the Privy Council, that the King, by letters patent, would confer on himself and his heirs, a tract of unoccupied crown land, adjoining Maryland and New Jersey, which he offered to accept in discharge of the obligation. He had more than one object in soliciting this grant. It would not only acquit his demand on the Government, but enable him to carry out designs which he had long fondly cherished; to provide a peaceful asylum for his persecuted brethren, as well as for the good and oppressed of every nation; to found a new empire on the pure and peaceable principles of Christianity; and so to conciliate the untutored savage by just and lenient measures, as to prepare him to receive the truths of the gospel. This "holy experiment" was warmly entered into by his manly generous mind, wearied with the pride, the selfishness, and cruelty of the old world.

His petition was referred to a Committee of the Privy Council, but strongly opposed by private interest and political bigotry. It was deemed an

Utopian scheme, likely, if countenanced, to prove an encouragement to the discontented, and dangerous to existing governments. After much difficulty and delay, however, the King acceded to his request, and in 1681 executed the patent, naming the new colony Pennsylvania, in honour of Admiral Penn.

The tract granted him was nearly 300 miles long and 160 broad, containing a surface little less than that of England. The entire region consisted either of dense forests or extensive pastures, where the native Indian reposed in safety, or roamed and hunted at pleasure: the river Delaware forming an excellent outlet to the sea.

The obtaining of this grant may be said to have been the great event of William Penn's life. From a despised and persecuted individual he became the sovereign of a little empire; and happily it was his chief desire to rule it in the fear of the Lord, for his glory, and for the good of the people. Many European settlers had acted with great injustice and cruelty towards the aboriginal inhabitants; taking possession of their lands without making them compensation, and treating them like wild beasts rather than as men. William Penn, on the contrary, though the King had made him a grant of the land, still considered the Indians as its proprietors, and purchased it of them on liberal terms: undertaking that all differences between his people and them should be referred to six white men and six Indians for settlement. This just course of procedure gave them entire satisfaction.

Some have been under the impression that the land of the Indians was obtained by William Penn, under the mere semblance of a purchase. That he gave no equivalent for the land. But it was stated, in evidence, before a Committee of the House of Commons, by Thomas Hodgekin,* that William Penn appears to have given about £20,000 to the Indians, and that they rapidly increased their price for land, until as early as 1682, two miles could not be obtained for what would at first purchase twenty. And this was at a time when land was valued so low that large tracts were given away by William Penn, who it was well known, so far from being enriched, was impoverished by his province. This he feelingly alludes to in an address to his friends in Pennsylvania, dated 4th mo., 29th, 1710, where he says, "And I cannot but think it hard measure, that while that has proved a land of freedom and flourishing, it should become to me by whose means it was principally made a country, the cause of grief, trouble and poverty."

That the advancement of the cause of universal righteousness, of peace on earth, and good will to men, was from the first his object in the "holy experiment," is forcibly set forth in the following letter:—

"My old friend, ************

"I could speak largely of God's dealings with me in getting this thing. What an inward exercise of

* North American Indians and Friends, p. 75.

faith and patience it cost me in passing. The travail was mine, as well as the debt and cost, through the envy of many, both professors, false friends and profane. My God hath given it me in the face of the world, and it is to hold it in true judgment, as a reward of my sufferings, and that is seen here, whatever some despisers may say or think. The place God hath given me, and I never felt judgment for the power I kept, but trouble for what I parted with. It is more than a worldly title or patent, that hath clothed me in this place. — Keep thy place: I am in mine, and have served the God of the whole earth, since I have been in it; nor am I sitting down in a greatness, that I have denied. I am day and night spending my life, my time, my money, and am not six-pence enriched by this greatness. Costs in getting, settling, transportation, and maintenance, now in a public manner at my own charge duly considered; to say nothing of my hazard, and the distance I am at from a considerable estate, and which is more, my dear wife and poor children.

"Well, — the Lord is a God of righteous judgment. Had I sought greatness, I had stayed at home, where the difference between what I am here, and was offered and could have been there, in power and wealth, is as wide as the places are. No, I came for the Lord's sake, and therefore have I stood to this day, well and diligent, and successful, blessed be his power. Nor shall I trouble myself to tell thee what I am to the people of this place, in travails, watchings, spendings, and my services every way, freely, (not like a selfish man) I have many witnesses. To conclude, it is now in Friends' hands. Through my travail, faith and patience it came. If Friends here keep to God, and in the justice, mercy, equity and fear of the Lord, their enemies will be their footstool. If not, their heirs and my heirs too will lose all, and desolation will follow; but blessed be the Lord, we are well and live in the dear love of God, and the fellowship of his tender heavenly Spirit, and our faith is for ourselves and one another, that the Lord will be with us a King, and a Counsellor for ever.

Thy ancient, though grieved friend,
William Penn."

Chester, 5th of the Twelfth
Month, 1682.

Abundant opportunity was soon offered for enriching himself from the grant of the king, as is plainly shown by the following testimony:

James Claypole, who became largely interested in the colony says, in a letter, "William Penn does not intend starting for Pennsylvania till next spring, and then it is like there will be many people ready to go from England, Scotland, and Ireland. He is offered great things; £6000 for a monopoly in trade which he refused, and for islands and particular places great sums of money; but he designs to do things equally between all parties, and I believe truly does aim more at justice and righteousness, and spreading of truth, than at his own particular gain." *

William Penn, in a letter to Robert Turner, alludes to the offer of £6000 as a great temptation, but says, "as the Lord had given him the province over all and great opposition, and that, as his mind was not so exercised to the Lord about any outward substance, he would not abuse his love, nor act unworthy of his providence, and so defile what came to him clean." "No," he goes on to say, "let the Lord guide me by his wisdom, and preserve me to honour His name, and serve His truth and people, that an example and standard may be set up to the nations."

The outline of his form of government, among many other excellent declarations, contains the following: "In reverence to God, the Father of light and spirits, I do for me and mine declare and establish, for the first fundamental of the government of my province, that every person residing therein shall enjoy the free profession of his or her faith and worship towards God, in such manner as every such person shall in conscience believe is most acceptable to Him. And so long as every such person useth not this Christian liberty to licentiousness or the destruction of others, viz., to speak loosely or contemptuously of God, Christ, the Holy Scriptures, or religion, or commit any moral evil or injury against others in their conversation, he or she shall be pro-

* Hazard, Annals of Pennsylvania, p. 522.

tected in the enjoyment of the aforesaid Christian liberty, by the civil magistrate."

The constitution which he himself prepared for the province, was admirable, and exceeded all the others which had been adopted in the American colonies. The celebrated John Locke, at the request of Lord Shaftesbury, drew up a form of government for Carolina; but it proved defective, and he had the candour to acknowledge the superiority of that of Pennsylvania.

While William Penn was busily engaged in preparing for the voyage to his new colony, his excellent mother died, — an event which deeply affected his feelings.

A deputy governor and three commissioners had already gone out to make the proper arrangements; several cargoes of emigrants and stores had been despatched; the colony had become popular; and early in 1682 the proprietor himself embarked, with about one hundred settlers, mostly his neighbours and friends, in the ship "Welcome," of three hundred tons burthen.

Before pursuing the account of the voyage, it may be proper to notice some of his late engagements at home. A few members of the Society of Friends, under pretence of a higher spirituality, and greater freedom from the limitations of their fellow men, had separated from the body, and endeavoured to draw others after them. They objected to the restraint of Church government, as an imposition upon conscience and an interference with Divine guidance.

William Penn treated the subject clearly and forcibly, in a tract, entitled "A Brief Examination of Liberty Spiritual;" as his friend R. Barclay had done before, in an excellent piece, called "Anarchy and Hierarchy equally refused and refuted." In 1681 William Penn was elected a member of the Royal Society then lately established; from the scientific labours of which he anticipated good moral as well as scientific results. The Friends of Bristol being subjected to severe persecution and great outrages, in attending their religious meetings, he appealed to the King and Parliament in their favour, and wrote them a kind, encouraging epistle. One of his last effusions at that time was the following memorable letter, full of tender affection and Christian advice, which he addressed to his wife and children before quitting England: —

"MY DEAR WIFE AND CHILDREN,

"My love, which neither sea nor land, nor death itself, can extinguish or lessen toward you, most endearly visits you with eternal embraces, and will abide with you for ever: and may the God of my life watch over you and bless you, and do you good in this world and for ever! — Some things are upon my spirit to leave with you in your respective capacities, as I am to the one a husband, and to the rest a father, if I should never see you more in this world.

"My dear wife, remember thou wast the love of my youth, and much the joy of my life; the most beloved, as well as most worthy of all my earthly comforts: and the reason of that love was more thy inward than thy outward excellencies, which yet were many. God knows, and thou knowest it, I can say it was a match of Providence's making; and God's image in us both was the first thing, and the most amiable and engaging ornament in our eyes. Now I am to leave thee, and that without knowing whether I shall ever see thee more in this world, take my counsel into thy bosom, and let it dwell with thee in my stead while thou livest.

"First: Let the fear of the Lord and a zeal and love to his glory dwell richly in thy heart; and thou wilt watch for good over thyself and thy dear children and family, that no rude, light or bad thing be committed: else God will be offended, and he will repent himself of the good he intends thee and thine.

"Secondly: Be diligent in meetings for worship and business; stir up thyself and others herein; it is thy duty and place: and let meetings be kept once a day in the family to wait upon the Lord, who has given us much time for ourselves. And my dearest, to make thy family matters easy to thee, divide thy time and be regular; it is easy and sweet: thy retirement will afford thee to do it; as in the morning to view the business of the house, and fix it as thou desirest, seeing all be in order; that by thy counsel all may move, and to thee render an account every evening. The time for work, for walking, for meals, may be certain, at least as near as may be: and grieve not thyself with careless servants; they will disorder thee: rather pay them, and let them go, if they will not be better by admonitions: this is best to avoid many words, which I know wound the soul and offend the Lord.

"Thirdly: Cast up thy income, and see what it daily amounts to; by which thou mayest be sure to have it in thy sight and power to keep within compass: and I beseech thee to live low and sparingly, till my debts are paid; and then enlarge as thou seest it convenient. Remember thy mother's example, when thy father's public-spiritedness had worsted his estate, which is my case. I know thou lovest plain things, and art averse to the pomps of the world; a nobility natural to thee. I write not as doubtful, but to quicken thee, for my sake, to be vigilant herein; knowing that God will bless thy care, and thy poor children and thee for it. My mind is wrapt up in a saying of thy father's, 'I desire not riches, but to owe nothing;' and truly that is wealth, and more than enough to live, is a snare attended with many sorrows. I need not bid thee be humble, for thou art so; nor meek and patient, for it is much of thy natural disposition: but I pray thee be oft in retirement with the Lord, and guard against encroaching friendships. Keep them at arm's end; for it is giving away our power, aye, and self too, into the possession of another; and that which might seem engaging in the beginning, may prove a yoke and burden too hard and heavy in the end. Wherefore keep dominion over thyself, and let thy children, good meetings and Friends, be the pleasure of thy life.

"Fourthly: And now, my dearest, let me recommend to thy care my dear children; abundantly beloved of me, as the Lord's blessings, and the sweet pledges of our mutual and endeared affection. Above all things endeavour to breed them up in the love of virtue, and that holy plain way of it which we have lived in, that the world in no part of it get into my family. I had rather they were homely than finely bred as to outward behaviour; yet I love sweetness mixed with gravity, and cheerfulness tempered with sobriety. Religion in the heart leads into this true civility, teaching men and women to be mild and courteous in their behaviour, an accomplishment worthy indeed of praise.

"Fifthly: Next breed them up in a love one of another: tell them it is the charge I left behind me; and that it is the way to have the love and blessings of God upon them; also what his portion is, who hates, or calls his brother fool. Sometimes separate them, but not long; and allow them to send and give each other small things to endear one another with. Once more I say, tell them it was my counsel they should be tender and affectionate one to another. For their learning be liberal. Spare no cost; for by such parsimony all is lost that is saved: but let it be useful knowledge, such as is consistent with Truth and godliness, not cherishing a vain conversation or idle mind; but ingenuity mixed with industry is good for the body and mind too. I recommend the useful parts of mathematics, as building houses or ships, measuring, surveying, dialling, navigation; but agriculture is especially in my eye: let my children be husbandmen and house-wives; it is industrious, healthy, honest and of good example: like Abraham and the holy ancients, who pleased God and obtained a good report. This leads to consider the works of God and nature, of things that are good, and diverts the mind from being taken up with the vain arts and inventions of a luxurious world. It is commendable in the princes of Germany and the nobles of that empire, that they have all their children instructed in some useful occupation. Rather keep an ingenious person in the house to teach them, than send them to schools, too many evil impressions being commonly received there. Be sure to observe their genius, and do not cross it as to learning: let them not dwell too long on one thing; but let their change be agreeable, and all their diversions have some little bodily labour in them. When grown big, have most care for them; for then there are more snares both within and without. When marriageable, see that they have worthy persons in their eye, of good life, and good fame for piety and understanding. I need no wealth, but sufficiency; and be sure their love be dear, fervent and mutual, that it may be happy for them. I choose not they should be married to earthly, covetous kindred. And of cities and towns of concourse beware; the world is apt to stick close to those who have lived and got wealth there: a country life and estate I like best for my children. I prefer a decent mansion, of an hundred pounds per annum, before ten thousand pounds in London, or such like place, in a way of trade. In fine, my dear, endeavour to breed them dutiful to the Lord, and his blessed light, truth and grace in their hearts, who is their Creator, and his fear will grow up with them. Teach a child, says the wise man, the way thou wilt have him to walk, and when he is old he will not forget it. Next, obedience to thee, their dear mother; and that not for wrath, but for conscience-sake; liberal to the poor, pitiful to the miserable, humble and kind to all; and may my God make thee a blessing, and give thee comfort in our dear children; and in age gather thee to the joy and blessedness of the just, where no death shall separate us, for ever!

"And now, my dear children, that are the gifts and mercies of the God of your tender father, hear my counsel, and lay it up in your hearts; love it more than treasure, and follow it, and you shall be blessed here, and happy hereafter.

"In the first place, remember your Creator in the days of your youth. It was the glory of Israel in the second of Jeremiah: and how did God bless Josiah because he feared him in his youth! and so he did Jacob, Joseph and Moses. O my dear children, remember, and fear and serve Him who made you and gave you to me and your dear mother; that you may live to him and glorify him in your generations!

6

"To do this, in your youthful days seek after the Lord, that you may find him; remembering his great love in creating you; that you are not beasts, plants or stones, but that he has kept you, and given you his grace within, and substance without, and provided plentifully for you. This remember in your youth, that you may be kept from the evil of the world: for in age it will be harder to overcome the temptations of it.

"Wherefore, my dear children, eschew the appearance of evil, and love and cleave to that in your hearts which shows you evil from good, and tells you when you do amiss, and reproves you for it. It is the light of Christ that he has given you for your salvation. If you do this and follow my counsel, God will bless you in this world, and give you an inheritance in that which shall never have an end. For the light of Jesus is of a purifying nature; it seasons those who love it and take heed to it; and never leaves such, till it has brought them to the city of God, that has foundations. O that ye may be seasoned with the gracious nature of it! hide it in your hearts, and flee, my dear children, from all youthful lusts; the vain sports, pastimes and pleasures of the world; redeeming the time, because the days are evil!—You are now beginning to live—what would some give for your time? Oh! I could have lived better, were I, as you, in the flower of youth. Therefore love and fear the Lord, keep close to meetings, and delight to wait on the Lord God of your father and mother, among his despised people, as we have done; and count it your honour to be members of that Society, and heirs of that living fellowship which is enjoyed among them, for the experience of which your father's soul blesseth the Lord for ever.

"Next: be obedient to your dear mother, a woman whose virtue and good name is an honour to you; for she hath been exceeded by none in her time for her plainness, integrity, industry, humanity, virtue and good understanding; qualities not usual among women of her worldly condition and quality. Therefore, honour and obey her, my dear children, as your mother, and your father's love and delight; nay love her too, for she loved your father with a deep and upright love, choosing him before all her many suitors: and though she be of a delicate constitution and noble spirit, yet she descended to the utmost tenderness and care for you, performing the painfulest acts of service to you in your infancy, as a mother and a nurse too. I charge you, before the Lord, honour and obey, love and cherish your dear mother.

"Next: betake yourselves to some honest, industrious course of life, and that not of sordid covetousness, but for example and to avoid idleness. And if you change your condition and marry, choose, with the knowledge and consent of your mother if living, or of guardians, or those that have the charge of you. Mind neither beauty nor riches, but the fear of the Lord, and a sweet and amiable disposition, such as you can love above all this world, and that may make your habitations pleasant and desirable to you.

"And being married, be tender, affectionate, patient and meek. Live in the fear of the Lord, and he will bless you and your offspring. Be sure to live within compass; borrow not, neither be beholden to any. Ruin not yourselves by kindness to others; for that exceeds the due bounds of friendship, neither will a true friend expect it. Small matters I heed not.

"Let your industry and parsimony go no further than for a sufficiency for life, and to make a provision for your children, and that in moderation, if the Lord gives you any. I charge you help the poor and needy; let the Lord have a voluntary share of your income for the good of the poor, both in our Society and others; for we are all his creatures; remembering that 'he that giveth to the poor lendeth to the Lord.'

"Know well your in-comings, and your out-goings may be better regulated. Love not money nor the world: use them only, and they will serve you; but if you love them you serve them, which will debase your spirits as well as offend the Lord.

"Pity the distressed, and hold out a hand of help to them; it may be your case; and as you mete to others God will mete to you again.

"Be humble and gentle in your conversation; of few words, I charge you; but always pertinent when you speak, hearing out before you attempt to answer, and then speaking as if you would persuade, not impose.

"Affront none, neither revenge the affronts that are done to you; but forgive, and you shall be forgiven of your Heavenly Father.

"In making friends consider well first; and when you are fixed be true, not wavering by reports nor deserting in affliction, for that becomes not the good and virtuous.

"Watch against anger, neither speak nor act in it; for, like drunkenness, it makes a man a beast, and throws people into desperate inconveniences.

"Avoid flatterers, for they are thieves in disguise; their praise is costly, designing to get by those they bespeak; they are the worst of creatures; they lie to flatter, and flatter to cheat; and which is worse, if you believe them you cheat yourselves most dangerously. But the virtuous, though poor, love, cherish and prefer. Remember David, who asking the Lord, 'Who shall abide in thy tabernacle? who shall dwell upon thy holy hill?' answers, 'He that walketh uprightly, worketh righteousness, and speaketh the truth in his heart; in whose eyes the vile person is contemned, but honoureth them that fear the Lord.'

"Next, my children, be temperate in all things; in your diet, for that is physic by prevention; it keeps, nay, it makes people healthy, and their generation sound. This is exclusive of the spiritual advantage it brings. Be also plain in your apparel; keep out that lust which reigns too much over some; let your virtues be your ornaments, remembering life is more than food, and the body than raiment. Let your furniture be simple and cheap. Avoid pride, avarice and luxury. Read my 'No Cross, no Crown.' There is instruction. Make your conversation with the most eminent for wisdom and piety; and shun all wicked men as you hope for the blessing of God and the comfort of your father's living and dying prayers. Be sure you speak no evil of any, no, not of the meanest; much less of your superiors, as magistrates, guardians, tutors, teachers and elders in Christ.

"Be no busy-bodies; meddle not with other folks' matters, but when in conscience and duty prest; for it procures trouble, and is ill manners, and very unseemly to wise men.

"In your families remember Abraham, Moses and Joshua, their integrity to the Lord; and do as you have them for your examples.

"Let the fear and service of the living God be encouraged in your houses, and that plainness, sobriety and moderation in all things as becometh God's chosen people; and as I advise you, my beloved children, do you counsel yours, if God should give you any. Yea, I counsel and command them as my posterity, that they love and serve the Lord God with an upright heart, that he may bless you and yours from generation to generation.

"And as for you, who are likely to be concerned in the government of Pennsylvania and my parts of East-Jersey, especially the first, I do charge you, before the Lord God and his holy angels, that you be lowly, diligent and tender, fearing God, loving the people, and hating covetousness. Let justice have its impartial course, and the law free passage. Though to your loss, protect no man against it; for you are not above the law, but the law above you. Live therefore the lives yourselves you would have the people live, and then you have right and boldness to punish the transgressor. Keep upon the square, for God sees you: therefore do your duty, and be sure you see with your own eyes, and hear with your own ears. Entertain no lurchers, cherish no informers for gain or revenge; use no tricks; fly to no devices to support or cover injustice; but let your hearts be upright before the Lord, trusting in him above the contrivances of men, and none shall be able to hurt or supplant.

"Oh! the Lord is a strong God, and he can do whatsoever he pleases; and though men consider it not, it is the Lord that rules and over-rules in the kingdoms of men, and he builds up and pulls down. I, your father, am the man that can say, He that trusts in the Lord, shall not be confounded. But God, in due time, will make his enemies be at peace with him.

"If you thus behave yourselves, and so become a terror to evil-doers, and a praise to them that do well, God, my God, will be with you in wisdom and a sound mind, and make you blessed instruments in his hand for the settlement of some of those desolate parts of the world, which my soul desires above all worldly honours and riches, both for you that go and you that stay; you that govern and you that are governed; that in the end you may be gathered with me to the rest of God.

"Finally, my children, love one another with a true endeared love, and your dear relations on both sides, and take care to preserve tender affection in your children to each other, often marrying within themselves, so as it be without the bounds forbidden in God's law, that so they may not, like the forgetting unnatural world, grow out of kindred and as cold as strangers; but as becomes a truly natural and Christian stock, you and yours after you may live in the pure and fervent love of God towards one another, as becoming brethren in the spiritual and natural relation.

"So, my God, that hath blessed me with his abundant mercies, both of this and the other and blessed life, be with you all, guide you by his counsel, bless you and bring you to his eternal glory! that you may shine, my dear children, in the firmament of God's power, with the blessed spirits of the just, that celestial family, praising and admiring him, the God and Father of it, for ever. For there is no God like unto him; the God of Isaac and of Jacob, the God of the prophets, the apostles and martyrs of Jesus, in whom I live for ever.

"So farewell to my thrice dearly beloved wife and children!

"Yours, as God pleaseth, in that which no waters can quench, no time forget, nor distance wear away, but remains for ever,

"WILLIAM PENN.

"Worminghurst, 4th of Sixth
Month, 1682."

To proceed with the notice of the voyage: — The "Welcome," with its cheerful passengers, had not long quitted Deal, before the small pox, in a virulent form, broke out among the ship's company. In the crowded vessel it spread rapidly, in spite of all precautions, and more than thirty deaths occurred within the nine weeks before the "Welcome" reached the promised land. The Governor was joyfully received, he treated all the people with kindness and goodwill, held his first assembly for the province, and established the great principle of religious liberty. He next proceeded to fix on a site between the Delaware and Skuylkill rivers for the capital city of the province, Philadelphia, and laid out the plan with great care and judgment.

The native tribes had always been objects of his special consideration: various purchases of land had already been made from them; and the Governor now proposed to meet them in a general conference, and to establish a treaty of perpetual peace and friendship between his people and them. A spot, then named Shackamaxon, on the western bank of the Delaware, had been formerly used by the Indians as a place of meeting on great occasions; and here, under an ancient spreading elm, the children of the forest on an appointed day, assembled to meet William Penn and his attendants. The proceedings were very simple but deeply interesting. The Governor, a handsome vigorous man, about thirty-eight years of age, distinguished by a blue silk sash round his waist, and provided with numerous presents spread on the ground, held in his hand a parchment roll, his officers and friends standing on each side and behind him. The Indians came in their forest costume, their bodies painted with bright colours, and their heads ornamented with trinkets and feathers. The principal chief, or sachem, put on his own head a chaplet, from which rose a small horn, the well-known emblem of supreme power; he was attended by other chiefs, by aged matrons, and many of his people, who formed a semicircle, and were mostly seated on the turf. He then informed the Governor, through an interpreter, that "the nations" were ready to hear him.

William Penn began by saying—that the great Spirit who made him and them, who ruled the heaven and the earth, and penetrated the innermost thoughts of men, knew that he and his friends had a hearty desire to live in peace and friendship with them, and to serve them to the utmost of their power. It was not their custom to use hostile weapons against their fellow creatures, and therefore they had come unarmed. Their object was not to do injury, and thus provoke the great Spirit, but to do good. They were then met on the broad pathway of sincerity and good-will, so that no advantage was to be taken on either side, but all was to be openness, brotherhood, and love. Unfolding the parchment, he explained to them, by an interpreter, the several articles of the treaty intended to cement their lasting union, and laid it on the ground, which he said should be common to both; concluding by declaring that he considered the Indians as the same flesh and blood, and of one body with the Christians; and presenting the parchment to the principal sachem, to be kept for future generations. The Indians listened to the address with silent gravity, but with great satisfaction; and an orator, on behalf of the rest, made a suitable reply, in which they pledged themselves to live in love with William Penn and his children as long as the sun and moon should endure.

This celebrated treaty and its faithful observance by each party have been extolled by both Christian and infidel writers: it is said to have been the only treaty made without an oath, and never broken. The whole conduct of William Penn toward the Indians was marked by justice and good-will; he not only paid them for their lands, but endeavoured in various ways to promote their welfare and improve their condition; and the Indian name of Onas or Penn has ever since been held in their grateful remembrance. While other colonies were kept in terror by bloody wars with the Indians, the unarmed inhabitants of Pennsylvania dwelt in peace and security.

The Indian tribes that met William Penn at thi famous treaty, are generally supposed to have been chiefly of the Lenni Lenape or Delaware stock, with some Mingoes, and other Susquehanna tribes, who came to solicit his friendship. The manner in which this and other treaties were conducted, is described by Penn in his letter to "The free society of Traders." He says "The order of the Indians is this; the King sits in the middle of an half moon, and hath his council, the old and wise, on each hand: behind them, or at a little distance, sit the younger fry in the same figure. Having consulted and resolved their business, the King ordered one of them to speak to me; he stood up, came to me, and in the name of his King saluted me, then took me by the hand and told me he was ordered by his King to speak to me, and that now it was not he, but the King that spoke, because what he should say was the King's mind. Having thus introduced the matter, he fell to the bounds of the land they had agreed to dispose of, and the price. During the time that this person spoke, not a man of them was observed to whisper or smile; the old, grave; the young, reverent in their deportment; they speak little, but fervently, and with elegancy. I have never seen more natural sagacity, considering them without the help, I was going to say, the spoil of tradition, and he will deserve the name of wise, that outwits them in any treaty about a thing they understand. When the purchase was agreed upon, great promises past between us of kindness and good neighbourhood, and that the English and Indians must live in love as long as the sun gave light—which done, another made a speech to the

Indians in the name of all the Sachamakers or Kings; first to tell them what was done; next to charge and command them, to love the Christians, and particularly live in peace with me, and the people under my government.— That many governors had been in the river, but that no governor had come himself to live and stay here before; and having now such an one, that had treated them well, they should never do him or his any wrong — at every sentence of which they shouted and said amen in their way."—

It is to be regretted that the authentic particulars preserved of the great treaty are very limited.

The place at which it was held, is now called Kensington, and is included within the thickly built parts of the city of Philadelphia A small marble monument marks the spot where stood the noble treaty elm tree, which was blown down in the year 1810. Much of the wood was preserved and made into various useful little articles to be kept as memorials of "unbroken faith." It is said that during the revolutionary war, the British general who was quartered at Kensington, so respected it, that when the soldiers were cutting down every tree for firewood, he placed a sentinel under it, that not a branch might be touched.

Governor Gordon, at a treaty held at Conestoga in 1728 with several nations of Indians who resided on the Susquehanna, thus alludes to the chief articles of Penn's treaty in a speech which he delivered to them.

"My brethren! — you have been faithful to your

leagues with us. Your leagues with William Penn and his governors are in writing on record, that our children and our children's children may have them in everlasting remembrance. And we know that you preserve the memory of these things amongst you by telling them to your children, and they again to the next generation, so that they remain stamped on your minds, never to be forgotten. The chief heads or strongest links of this chain I find are these nine, to wit:

"1st. That all William Penn's people, or Christians, and all the Indians, should be brethren, as the children of one father, joined together as with one heart, one head and one body.

"2d. That all paths should be open and free to both Christians and Indians.

"3d. That the doors of the Christians' houses should be open to the Indians, and the houses of the Indians opened to the Christians, and that they should make each other welcome as their friends.

"4th. That the Christians should not believe any false rumors or reports of the Indians, nor the Indians believe any such rumors or reports of the Christians, but should first come as brethren to inquire of each other; and that both Christians and Indians, when they have any such false reports of their brethren, should bury them as in a bottomless pit.

"5th. That if the Christians hear any ill news that may be to the hurt of the Indians, or the Indians hear any such ill news, that may be to the injury of the Christians, they should acquaint each other with it speedily as true friends and brethren.

"6th. That the Indians should do no manner of harm to the Christians nor to their creatures, nor the Christians do any hurt to the Indians, but each treat each other as brethren.

"7th. But as there are wicked people in all nations, if either Indians or Christians should do any harm to each other, complaint should be made of it by the persons suffering, that right might be done, and when satisfaction is made the injury or wrong should be forgot, and be buried as in a bottomless pit.

"8th. That the Indians should in all things assist the Christians, and the Christians assist the Indians against all wicked people that would disturb them.

"9th. And lastly, that both Christians and Indians should acquaint their children with this league and firm chain of friendship made between them, and that it should always be made stronger and stronger, and be kept bright and clean, without rust or spot, between our children and our children's children, while the creeks and rivers run, and while the sun, moon, and stars endure."

John Richardson, an eminent minister in the Society of Friends, who in the year 1701 was engaged in a religious visit to America, visited William Penn at his country house at Pennsbury Manor, and there met a tribe of Indians who came to renew their treaty of alliance and friendship. He says "it was done in much calmness of temper and in an amicable way," and that "they never first broke covenant with any people," for "as one of them said, and smote his hand on his head three times, they did not make them there in their heads, but smiting his hand three times on his breast, said, they made them there in their hearts."

He had some religious interviews with the Indians, and remarks, "I have often thought and said when I was among them, that generally my spirit was easy, and I did not feel that power of darkness to oppress me, as I have done in many places among the people called Christians."

On one occasion he visited their wigwams with an interpreter, and exhorting them as one "who came from a far distant country, with a message from the Great Man above" to cease from evil things for which He would be angry with them. When the interpreter explained the discourse to them, they wept, and tears ran down their naked bodies, and they smote their hands upon their breasts, and said something to the interpreter. John Richardson asked what they said — the interpreter replied, "they said all that I had delivered to them was good, and except the Great Man had sent me, I could not have told them these things." I desired the interpreter to ask them, how they knew what I said was good; they replied and smote their hands on their breasts, the Good Man here (meaning in their hearts) told them what I had said was all good. They manifested much love to me in their way, and I believe the love of God is to them and all people in the day of their visitation."—

In the last interview William Penn had with the

Indians in 1701, he told them "That he had always loved, and been kind to them, and ever should continue so to be, not through any politic design or on account of self interest, but from a most real affection; and he desired them in his absence, to cultivate friendship with those whom he should leave behind in authority; as they would always, in some degree, continue to be so to them as himself had ever been; lastly, that he had charged the members of the council, and he then also renewed the same charge, that they should in all respects be kind to them, and entertain them with all courtesy and demonstrations of good will, as himself had ever done."

At a council held in Philadelphia, 6th mo., 14th, 1715, at which James Logan, Isaac Norris, Richard Hill, and others of the council were present, Sassoonan, chief of the Delawares, rose and said "That William Penn had, at his first coming, made a clear and open road all the way to the Indians, that they desired the same might be kept open, and that all obstructions should be removed, all of which on their side they would take care." He then presented a belt of wampum and added, "That they desired the peace which had been made should be so firm, that they and we should join hand in hand so firmly, that nothing, even the greatest tree, should be able to divide them asunder." Laying down a second belt, he added "That in the last counsel which they held with us, they spoke concerning the sun, by whose influence they had lived in warmth and plenty, from the beginning; that they now desired the same happiness might be continued to them with us in the firmest peace; and that it might last as long as the sun should endure; that when any clouds interpose between them and the sun, it brings coolness and is unpleasant; the same will be, if any cloud should arise between them and us, and therefore they desire, if any thing of that kind appear, it may be dissipated without delay."

At a treaty held with the Six Nations at Philadelphia, in 1742, Canassatego, chief of the Onondagoes, said, "We are all very sensible of the kind regard which that good man, William Penn, had for all the Indians."

In 1749, a council was held during the administration of James Hamilton, with the Senecas and other Indians in Philadelphia, on which occasion Ogaustash, thus expresses himself: —

"We recommend it to the governor to tread in the steps of those wise people who have held the reins of government before him, in being good and kind to the Indians. Do, brother, make it your study to consult the interest of our nations; as you have so large an authority, you can do us much good or harm; we would, therefore, engage your influence and affections for us, that the same harmony and mutual affections may subsist during your government, which so happily subsisted in former times, — nay from the first settlement of this province by our good friend the great William Penn."

So long as Friends continued to have a controlling influence in conducting the government of Pennsylvania, a kind and conciliatory treatment was maintained towards the Indians, and the friendship which existed between them was but little, if at all interrupted. The upright and judicious management of James Logan, the confidential friend and secretary of William Penn, who was long the commissioner for land affairs, contributed powerfully to the preservation of the friendship and alliance of the Indians. But after his death in 1751, a different line of policy was soon commenced, and, by the elections, Friends were excluded from their majority in the Assembly.

The peaceable mode in which the government of the province had been conducted was now departed from, and the abuses committed against the Indians in trading, and in taking possession of their land, not being properly redressed, an open rupture soon took place, attended with the most calamitous results.

No longer able to control the movements of government, Friends nevertheless continued to exert their influence for reconciliation, and it is stated that in 1756, an association was formed "For gaining and preserving peace with the Indians by pacific measures" — many thousand pounds were raised by subscription, and expended chiefly in presents to the Indians in order to conciliate them, and sometimes with a view to prevail on them to seek out and release the settlers whom they had taken prisoners. These exertions seem to have had a most salutary effect, and indeed appear to have been mainly instrumental in restoring peace to the province.

That the Indians more than half a century after

the departure of William Penn, retained a clear sense of that bond of faith, made, as they so forcibly describe, in the heart, and not alone in the head, is shown by the speech of one of the Delaware chiefs at a treaty held in 1756, after they had suffered many grievous injuries from their professing Christian neighbours. On this occasion he says, "We are rejoiced to hear from you, that you are willing to renew the old good understanding, and that you call to mind the first treaty of friendship made by Onas, our great friend, deceased, with our forefathers, when himself and his people first came over here. We take hold of these treaties with both our hands, and desire you will do the same, that a good understanding and true friendship may be re-established. Let us both take hold of these treaties, with all our strength, we beseech you. We on our side will certainly do it."—

Another Indian said, "I wish the same good spirit that possessed the good old man, William Penn, who was a friend to the Indians, may inspire the people of this province at this time."

It was an observation of William Penn's with respect to the Indians, "Do not abuse them, but let them have but justice, and you win them." That this observation was correct, has been abundantly shown. The Indians were won — won by justice and kind treatment, and ever evinced a desire to show their grateful sense of it, by rendering kind services to the colonists. "We have done better" said one of the settlers in 1684, "than if with the proud Spaniards, we had gained the mines of Potosi. We may make the ambitious heroes whom the world admires, blush for their shameful victories. To the poor, dark souls round about us, we teach their rights as men." The peaceful and even affectionate conduct of the Indians toward Friends, is another striking result of the benefit of the course adopted towards them, so that, although unarmed, and in a defenceless condition as regarded their personal safety, they lived among them in entire security. "As in other countries," says Richard Townsend, "the Indians were exasperated by hard treatment, which has been the foundation of much bloodshed, so the contrary treatment here, by our worthy proprietor, hath produced their love and affection." In a letter of one of the early settlers, already noticed, it is stated that "the Indians were even rendered our benefactors and protectors; — without any carnal weapons we entered the land and inhabited therein, as safe as if there had been thousands of garrisons." "This little state," says Oldmixon, "subsisted in the midst of six Indian Nations, without so much as a militia for a defense." *

Heckewelder, in his history of the Indian nations, mentions their care to preserve, by means of strings and belts of wampum, the memory of their treaties, and especially those they made with William Penn. He says, "They frequently assembled together in the woods, in some shady spot, as nearly as possible similar to those where they used to meet their

* See Appendix.

brother Miquon, and there lay all his words and speeches, with those of his descendants, on a blanket or clean piece of bark, and with great satisfaction go successively over the whole. This practice, which I have repeatedly witnessed, continued until the year 1780, when the disturbances which took place put an end to it probably for ever."

As a further evidence that the Christian treatment of William Penn had made a deep and durable impression on the hearts of the Indians, we quote a letter of Corn Planter, Chief of the Senecas, addressed "To the children of Onas, who first settled in Pennsylvania.'

"BROTHERS.—The Seneca nation see that the Great Spirit intends that they shall not continue to live by hunting, and they look around on every side, and inquire who it is that shall teach them what is best for them to do. Your fathers have dealt honestly and fairly with our fathers, and they have charged us to remember it; and we think it right to tell you that we wish our children to be taught the same principles by which your fathers were guided in their councils.

"Brothers.—We have too little wisdom among us, we cannot teach our children what we perceive their situation requires them to know, and we therefore ask you to instruct some of them; we wish them to be instructed to read and write, and such other things as you teach your own children; and especially to teach them to love peace.

"Brothers.—We desire of you to take under your care two Seneca boys, and teach them as your own; and in order that they may be satisfied to remain with you, and be easy in their minds, that you will take with them the son of our interpreter, and teach him also according to his desire.

"Brothers.—You know that it is not in our power to pay you for the education of these three boys; and, therefore, you must, if you do this thing, look up to God for your reward.

"Brothers.—You will consider of this request, and let us know what you determine to do. If your hearts are inclined towards us, and you will afford our nation this great advantage, I will send my son as one of the boys to receive your instruction, and at the time which you shall appoint.

his
CORN PLANTER." ×
mark.

Signed, February 10th, 1791.

The treatment of the aborigines of our country being to the present day a question of deep interest, it has been considered proper to introduce some of the foregoing particulars, though not closely connected with the times of our memoir, to show that the peaceable principles of Christianity, practically carried out, are the surest means of promoting their improvement, of disarming their warlike feelings, and of enabling others, whom the cause of human progress and civilization may lead into their wide domain, to dwell in safety and peace.

That the great and good Spirit, the "God of the spirit of all flesh," dwells as well in the heart of the Indian, as in that of his white neighbour, cannot be safely questioned; that the benefits of the dispensation of "peace on earth, and good will to men," under which it is our privilege to live, were intended as well for them, as for professing Christians, will probably be denied by few—may it, therefore, be our fervent prayer, that the knowledge of this glorious Gospel dispensation may spread and cover the earth, as the waters do the sea, and the hearts of all, of every nation, may be so turned to one another, that each, in the bond of peace, may call "every man his brother."

Returning to the regular order of our memoir, it appears that the time of the Governor was much occupied with the concerns of his rising province. He surveyed the territory, built bridges, enacted laws, settled differences, founded schools, laid out towns and cities, and saw an industrious, thriving population of nearly six thousand English, beside Germans and Dutch, settled around him in comfort and prosperity. Before his death, the rapidly increasing inhabitants had amounted to sixty thousand. In the midst of his secular labours he did not forget his religious duties; but established many meetings for worship, often ministered in them himself, travelling in this service through various parts, and introducing a system of wholesome Church government. After remaining among his people, as a ruler and a father, for nearly two years, he thought it best to return to England. The boundary between Pennsylvania and Maryland required settlement at home; persecution had broken out with renewed violence; and unfounded reports endangered his own reputation. He embarked in the summer of 1684, and had a prosperous voyage.

On his arrival in England, the same objects chiefly engaged his attention, and called him frequently to the Court. To stay if possible the cruel arm of persecution, he earnestly pleaded with the King, and published a forcible appeal to the public. As respected the boundary between his own province and Maryland, whose proprietor, Lord Baltimore, refused reasonable terms, he was ultimately successful.

## CHAPTER VI. 1685–1695.

JAMES II. LIBERATES FRIENDS FROM PRISON; W. PENN'S INFLUENCE WITH HIM USED IN FAVOR OF THE OPPRESSED—RENDERS HIMSELF SUSPECTED AND UNPOPULAR—POPPLE'S LETTER, AND REPLY OF W. PENN — EPISTLE TO FRIENDS—THE REVOLUTION — W. PENN ARRESTED, BUT ACQUITTED THREE TIMES — SECLUDES HIMSELF FOR TWO YEARS — WRITES "REFLECTIONS AND MAXIMS"—AGAIN HONORABLY ACQUITTED — HIS WIFE DIES — TRIBUTE TO HER WORTH — PENNSYLVANIA TAKEN AWAY, BUT RESTORED TO HIM — HIS DOCTRINAL VIEWS.

In about six months after William Penn's return to England, Charles II. died, leaving at least one thousand four hundred Friends in prison, many of whom had been long and cruelly detained on account of their religious principles. Not less than fifteen thousand families of different denominations are said to have been brought to ruin, and five thousand persons to have died, for the same cause, in his reign. All the Friends were set at liberty by royal proclamation, as were also John Bunyan and some other dissenters of eminence. W. Penn, however, wished the new King to act more in concert with his Parliament than his own despotic disposition inclined him to do. He had always shown himself favourable to toleration, and while he now openly professed the Roman Catholic faith, he publicly disclaimed arbitrary principles of government, promising to respect the rights of all, and to maintain the Church of England as by law established; yet many Protestants, who had dreaded his advent to power, alarmed by the revocation of the edict of Nantes, and the massacres in France, doubted the sincerity of his motives. William Penn, who had always been on intimate terms with James, became, like him, an object of public suspicion; which was increased by his frequent presence at Court, and by the influence which he had with his royal patron—though he used it in favour of the oppressed. One of the first persons whom he attempted to serve was the celebrated John Locke, with whom he had long been on friendly terms, and who was then an exile in Holland, on account of his independent conduct: but Locke declined to accept the pardon offered him.

The insurrection under the Duke of Monmouth was soon quelled, and was followed by the judicial barbarities of Jefferies. Macaulay has attempted to connect William Penn with some of those vindictive atrocities, but the charge is wholly destitute of proof. His conduct both in America and in England was, however, strangely assailed and unjustly stigmatized. He was represented as a Jesuit or Papist in disguise; even some of his own friends became uneasy at the reports which were circulated; and Dr. Tillotson told him plainly of his own fears respecting him. An interesting correspondence followed. William Penn expressed his grief at finding that any of his friends credited such reports, asserting that he neither exchanged letters with Romish priests, nor was even acquainted with any such. But, though not a Romanist, he avowed himself a Catholic in the true sense of the word,—a Christian, whose creed was the New Testament; and that he could not refuse that liberty to others which he claimed for himself; believing that faith, piety, and providence were a better security than force, and that if truth could not succeed with her own weapons, all others would fail her. Tillotson candidly acknowledged his conviction that the reports were groundless. The Duke of Buckingham, having written a work in favour of liberty of conscience, and being attached to William Penn, publicly defended him.

The state of affairs in Pennsylvania at this time being not very satisfactory, made him earnestly desirous to return thither; but a strong sense of duty detained him in England, and he continued to plead zealously for full religious liberty. In a tract, entitled "Fiction found out," he says, in his usual manly style, "I have this defence for my religion and conduct: First, that the grace of God within me, and the Scriptures without me, are the foundation and declaration of my faith and religion: let any man get better if he can. Secondly, that the profession I make of this religion, is in the same way and manner that I have used for almost eighteen years past. Thirdly, that my civil conduct, I humbly bless my God, has been with peace on earth, and good will to all men, from the King on the throne, to the beggar on the dunghill."

In 1686 he undertook another journey to the continent on religious service; and the King, having learned his intention, requested him to see the Prince of Orange, and endeavour to gain his approval of a general toleration and the removal of all religious tests in England. Of the former of these the Prince approved, but he was opposed to withdrawing the tests; and in these views he was encouraged by Dr. Burnet, then at the Hague. Proceeding to Amsterdam, W. Penn formed an intimacy with W. Sewell, a learned man, then employed in translating the "No cross no Crown" into Dutch. He next travelled into Germany as a minister of the gospel; of which service he briefly says, the Lord blessed him with his glorious presence and power. He became interested in the condition of several English and Scotch refugees, to whom on his return home he rendered important service, by pleading their cause with the King.

He next visited, as a minister, some of the midland and northern counties of England, and the King making a tour in that direction, they occasionally met. The meetings at Bristol, Chester, and some other places, were very large, and at one or more the King appears to have been present. They were at Oxford together: and here James committed, on the members of Magdalen College, one of those unjust acts, which proved at once his arbitrary and his Romanising disposition. William Penn remonstrated with him against it, and acted as a sort of mediator between the King and the Fellows of the College.

He was however unsuccessful, and the latter, though he pleaded their cause, did not relish his views of opening the university to all religious bodies, and joined in the outcry against him, as being inclined to Popery. James resolved to pursue his own unwise course, and did not repent till it was too late.

William Penn's position at this time was extremely delicate and critical. His close intimacy with an unconstitutional monarch, a Papist and a despot, who yet professed to favour liberty of conscience, which he himself decidedly approved, rendered him an object of great suspicion, unpopularity, and misrepresentation, on both political and religious grounds; yet there is ample reason to believe that he endeavoured to maintain a clear conscience in all respects, that he abhorred both tyranny and Popery, and that the charges brought against his motives and character at that time, and repeated in our own day, are wholly destitute of solid foundation. Abundant is the evidence that he exerted his influence to help the oppressed and to prevent violent measures.

The King, however, seemed infatuated. Early in 1688, contrary to the advice of William Penn and some others, he resolved to take the power again into his own hands, as his brother Charles II had done: and he not only issued a proclamation, a second time suspending the execution of all penal laws in matters ecclesiastical, but also, by an Order of Council, he, directed the proclamation "to be read in all churches." Archbishop Sancroft and six bishops presented a petition against the reading of the document, but in vain; the King construed their proceedings into an insult, and sent them to the Tower, from which they were soon after liberated by process of law. William Penn now became more unpopular than ever; he was even suspected of having a hand in these unconstitutional measures; and Jesuits being openly received at Court, he was charged with encouraging them.

On this subject, William Popple, Secretary to the Board of Trade and Plantations, addressed him a letter, in which he says, "If I had not that particular respect for you which I sincerely profess, yet I could not but be much affected that any man who had deservedly acquired so fair a reputation as you have had, whose integrity and veracity had always been reputed spotless, and whose charity had been continually exercised in serving others at the dear expense of his time, his strength, and his estate, without any other recompense than what results from the consciousness of doing good: I say, I could not but be much affected to see any such person fall innocently and undeservedly, under such unjust reproaches, as you have done."

Alluding then to the charges brought against him, "that under the guise of promoting liberty of conscience, he had connived with King James to settle Popery in the nation, that "he was a Jesuit," that "his professions for the establishment of religious liberty were insincere," he most earnestly and affectionately exhorts him to come out with a public vindication of his innocence, that these scandalous imputations might no longer lie upon him, and says, "I beg of you, by all the tender efficacy that friendship, either mine, or that of your friends and relations together, can have upon you; by the due regard which humanity and even Christianity obliges you to have to your reputation; by the cause of universal religion and eternal truth; to serve your King, your country and your religion, by such a public vindication of your honour, as your own prudence, upon these suggestions, will show you to be most necessary, and most expedient."

To this friendly and impressive appeal, William Penn made the following reply :—

"Worthy Friend,

"It is now above twenty years, I thank God, that I have not been very solicitous what the world thought of me. For, since I have had the knowledge of religion from a principle in myself, the first and main point with me has been, to approve myself in the sight of God, through patience and well-doing. So that the world has not had weight enough with me, to suffer its good opinion to raise me, or its ill opinion to deject me. And if that had been the only motive or consideration, and not the desire of a good friend in the name of many others, I had been as silent to thy letter, as I use to be to the idle and malicious shams of the times. But, as the laws of friendship are sacred, with those that value that relation, so I confess this to be a principal one with me, not to deny a friend the satisfaction he desires, when it may be done without offence to a good conscience.

"The business chiefly insisted upon, is my Popery, and endeavours to promote it. I do say then, and that with all sincerity, That I am not only no Jesuit, but no Papist. And which is more, I never had any temptation upon me to be one, either from doubts in my own mind about the way I profess, or from the discourses or writings of any of that religion. And in the presence of Almighty God, I do declare, that the King did never once, directly or indirectly, attack me, or tempt me upon that subject, the many years that I have had the advantage of a free access to him; so unjust, as well as sordidly false, are all those stories of the town.

"The only reason that I can apprehend, they have to repute me a Roman Catholic, is, my frequent going to Whitehall, a place no more forbid to me than to the rest of the world, who yet, it seems, find much fairer quarter. I have almost continually had one business or other there for our Friends, whom I ever served with a steady solicitation, through all times, since I was of their communion. I had also a great many personal good offices to do, upon a principle of charity for people of all persuasions, thinking it a duty to improve the little interest I had for the good of those that needed it, especially the poor. I might add something of my own affairs too, though I must own, if I may without vanity, that they have ever had the least share of my thoughts or pains, or else they would not have still depended as they yet do.

"But because some people are so unjust, as to render instances of my Popery, or rather hypocrisy, for so it would be in me, it is fit I contradict them as particularly as they accuse me. I say then, solemnly, that I am so far from having been bred at St. Omer's, and having received orders at Rome, that I never was at either place, nor do I know any body there; nor had I ever a correspondence with any body in those places, which is another story invented against me. And, as for my officiating in the King's chapel, or any other, it is so ridiculous, as well as untrue, that besides, that nobody can do it but a priest, and that I have been married to a woman of some condition above sixteen years, which no priest can be, by any dispensation whatever; I have not so much as looked into any chapel of the Roman religion, and consequently not the King's, though a common curiosity warrants it daily to people of all persuasions.

"And, once for all, I do say, That I am a Protestant dissenter, and to that degree such, that I challenge the most celebrated Protestant of the English Church, or any other, on that head, be he layman or clergyman, in public or in private. For, I would have such people know, it is not impossible, for a true Protestant dissenter to be dutiful, thankful and serviceable to the King, though he be of the Roman Catholic communion. We hold not our property or protection from him by our persuasion, and, therefore, his persuasion should not be the measure of our allegiance. I am sorry to see so many who seem fond of the reformed religion, by their disaffection to him, recommend it so illy. Whatever practices of Roman Catholics we might reasonably object against, and no doubt but such there are, yet he has disclaimed and reprehended those ill things by his declared opinion against persecution; by the ease in which he actually indulges all dissenters, and by the confirmation he offers in Parliament, for the security of the Protestant religion and liberty of conscience. And, in his honour, as well as in my own defence, I am obliged in conscience to say, that he has ever declared to me, it was his opinion, and on all occasions, when Duke, he never refused me the repeated proofs of it, as often as I had any poor sufferers for conscience-sake to solicit his help for.

"But some may be apt to say, Why not any body else as well as I? Why must I have the preferable access to other dissenters, if not a Papist? I answer, I know not that it is so. But, this I know, that I have made it my province and business; I have followed and prest it, I took it for my calling and station, and have kept it above these sixteen years, and, which is more, if I may say it without vanity or reproach, wholly at my own charges too. To this let me add the relation my father had to this King's service, his particular favour in getting me released out of the tower of London in '69, my father's humble request to him upon his death-bed, to protect me from the inconveniences and troubles my persuasion might expose me to, and his friendly promise to do it, and exact performance of it, from the moment I addressed myself to him. I say, when all this is considered, any body that has the least pretence to good nature, gratitude, or generosity, must needs know how to interpret my access to the King. Perhaps some will be ready to say, This is not all, nor is this yet a fault, but that I have been an adviser to other matters disgustful to the kingdom, and which tend to the overthrow of the Protestant religion, and the liberties of the people. A likely thing, indeed, that a Protestant dissenter, who, from fifteen years old, has been, at times, a sufferer in his father's family, in the university, and by the government, for being so, should design the destruction of the Protestant religion. This is just as probable as it is true, that I died a Jesuit, six years ago, in America. Will men still suffer such stuff to pass upon them? Is any thing more foolish as well as false, than that, because I am often at Whitehall, therefore, I must be the author of all that is done there, that does not please abroad. But, supposing some such things to have been done, pray tell me, if I am bound to oppose any thing that I am not called to do? I never was a member of council, cabinet, or committee, where the affairs of the kingdom are transacted. I have had no office, or trust, and consequently, nothing can be said to be done by me, nor for that reason, could I lie under any test or obligation, to discover my opinion of public acts of state, and, therefore, neither can any such acts, nor my silence about them, in justice, be made my crime. Volunteers are blanks and cyphers in all governments. And, unless calling at Whitehall once a day, upon many occasions, or my not being turned out of nothing, for that no office is, be the evidence of my compliance in disagreeable things, I know not what else can with any truth, be alleged against me. However, one thing I know, that I have every where most religiously observed, and endeavoured in conversation with persons of all ranks and opinions, to allay heats and moderate extremities, even in the politics. It is below me to be more particular, but I am sure it has been my endeavour, that if we could not all meet upon a religious bottom, at least we might upon a civil one, the good of England; which is the common interest of King and people. That he might be great by justice, and we free by obedience; distinguishing rightly on the one hand, between duty and slavery; and, on the other, between liberty and licentiousness.

"But, alas! I am not without my apprehensions of the cause of this behaviour towards me, and in this, I perceive we agree; I mean my constant zeal for an impartial liberty of conscience. But, if that be it, the cause is too good to be in pain about. I ever understood that to be the natural right of all men; and that he that had a religion without it, his religion was none of his own. For, what is not the religion of a man's choice, is the religion of him that imposes it. So that liberty of conscience is the

9

first step to have a religion. This is no new opinion with me. I have written many apologies within the last twenty years to defend it, and that impartially. Yet I have as constantly declared, that bounds ought to be set to this freedom, and that morality was the best; and that as often as that was violated, under a pretence of conscience, it was fit the civil power should take place. Nor did I ever once think of promoting any sort of civil liberty of conscience for any body, which did not preserve the common Protestancy of the kingdom, and the ancient rights of the government. For, to say truth, the one cannot be maintained without the other.

"Upon the whole matter, I must say, I love England; I ever did so; and that I am not in her debt. I never valued time, money, nor kindred, to serve her and do her good. No party could ever bias me to her prejudice, nor any personal interest oblige me in her wrong. For, I always abhorred discounting private favours at the public cost.

"Would I have made my market of the fears and jealousies of people; when this King came to the crown, I had put twenty thousand pounds into my pocket, and an hundred thousand into my province. For mighty numbers of people were then upon the wing. But I waived it all, hoped for better times; expected the effects of the King's word for liberty of conscience, and happiness by it. And, till I saw my friends, with the kingdom, delivered from the legal bondage, which penal laws for religion had subjected them to, I could, with no satisfaction, think of leaving England; though much to my prejudice beyond sea, and at my great expense here; having in all this time, never had either office or pension; and always refusing the rewards or gratuities of those I have been able to oblige.

"If, therefore, an universal charity, if the asserting an impartial liberty of conscience, if doing to others as one would be done by, and an open avowing and steady practising of these things, in all times, to all parties, will justly lay a man under the reflection of being a Jesuit or Papist, of any rank, I must not only submit to the character, but embrace it too; and I care not who knows, that I can wear it with more pleasure, than it is possible for them with any justice to give it me. For these are corner-stones and principles with me; and I am scandalized at all buildings that have them not for their foundation. For religion itself is an empty name without them, a whited wall, a painted sepulchre, no life or virtue to the soul; no good or example to one's neighbour. Let us not flatter ourselves; we can never be the better for our religion, if our neighbour be the worse for it. Our fault is, we are apt to be mighty hot upon speculative errors, and break all bounds in our resentments; but we let practical ones pass without remark, if not without repentance. As if a mistake about an obscure proposition of faith, were a greater evil than the breach of an undoubted precept. Such a religion the devils themselves are not without; for they have both faith and knowledge, but their faith doth not work by love, nor their knowledge by obedience. And, if this be their judgment, can it be our blessing? Let us not then think religion a litigious thing; or that Christ came only to make us good disputants, but that he came also to make us good livers. Sincerity goes further than capacity. It is charity that deservedly excels in the Christian religion; and happy would it be, if where unity ends, charity did begin, instead of envy and railing, that almost ever follow. It appears to me to be the way that God has found out, and appointed to moderate our differences, and make them at least harmless to society; and, therefore, I confess, I dare not aggravate them to wrath and blood. Our disagreement lies in our apprehension or belief of things; and if the common enemy of mankind had not the governing of our affections and passions, that disagreement would not prove such a canker as it is, to love and peace, in civil societies.

"He that suffers his difference with his neighbour about the other world, to carry him beyond the line of moderation in this, is the worse for his opinion, even though it be true. It is too little considered by Christians, that men may hold the truth in unrighteousness; that they may be orthodox, and not know what spirit they are of; so were the Apostles of our Lord; they believed in him, yet let a false zeal do violence to their judgment, and their unwarrantable heat contradict the great end of their Saviour's coming, love.

"Men may be angry for God's sake, and kill people too. Christ said it, and too many have practised it. But what sort of Christians must they be, I pray, that can hate in his name, who bids us love; and kill for his sake, that forbids killing; and commands love, even to enemies?

"Let not men or parties think to shift it off from themselves. It is not this principle, or that form, to which so great a defection is owing, but a degeneracy of mind from God. Christianity is not at heart, no fear of God in the inward parts. No awe of his Divine Omnipresence. Self prevails, and breaks out more or less, through all forms, but too plainly (pride, wrath, lust, avarice), so that though people say to God, Thy will be done, they do their own; which shows them to be true heathens, under a mask of Christianity, that believe without works, and repent without forsaking, busy for forms and the temporal benefits of them, while true religion, which is to visit the fatherless and the widow, and to keep ourselves unspotted from the world, goes barefoot, and, like Lazarus, is despised. Yet this was the definition the Holy Ghost gave of religion, before synods and councils had the meddling with it, and modelling of it. In those days bowels were a good part of religion, and that to the fatherless and widow at large. We can hardly now extend them to those of our own way. It was said by him that could not say amiss; Because iniquity abounds, the love of many waxeth cold. Whatsoever divides man's heart from God, separates it from his neighbour; and he that loves self more than God, can never love his neighbour as himself. For, as the

Apostle said, if we do not love him whom we have seen, how can we love God, whom we have not seen?

"O that we could see some men as eager to turn people to God, as they are to blow them up, and set them against one another. But, indeed, those only can have that pure and pious zeal, who are themselves turned to God, and have tasted the sweetness of that conversion, which is to power, not form; to godliness, not gain. Such as those bend their thoughts and pains to appease, not increase heats and animosities, to exhort people to look at home, sweep their own houses, and weed their own gardens. And, in no age or time, was there more need to set men at work in their own hearts, than this we live in, when so busy, wandering, licentious a spirit prevails. For, whatever some men may think, the disease of this kingdom is sin, impiety against God, and want of charity to men. And while this guilt is at our door, judgment cannot be far off.

"Now this being the disease, I will briefly offer two things for the cure of it. The first is, David's clean heart and right spirit, which he asked, and had of God. Without this we must be a chaos still; for the distemper is within; and our Lord said, All evil comes from thence. Set the inward man right, and the outward man cannot be wrong. That is the helm that governs the human vessel. And this nothing can do but an inward principle, the light and grace that came by Christ, who the Scriptures tell us, enlightens every one, and hath appeared to all men.

It is preposterous to think, that he who made the world, should show least care of the best part of it, our souls; no, he that gave us an outward luminary for our bodies, hath given us an inward one for our minds to act by. We have it; and it is our condemnation that we do not love it, and bring our deeds to it. It is by this we see our sins, are made sensible of them, sorry for them, and finally forsake them. And he that thinks to go to Heaven a nearer way, will, I fear, belate his soul, and be irreparably mistaken. There are but goats and sheep at last, whatever shapes we wear here. Let us not, therefore, dear friend, deceive ourselves. Our souls are at stake, God will not be mocked, what we sow we must expect to reap. There is no repentance in the grave; which shows, that if none there, then no where else. To sum up this divinity of mine; it is the light of Jesus in our souls, that gives us a true sight of ourselves, and that sight that leads us to repentance, which repentance begets humility, and humility that true charity, that covers a multitude of faults, which I call God's expedient against man's infirmity. The second remedy to our present distemper is this; since all of all parties profess to believe in God, Christ, the Spirit, and Scripture, that the soul is immortal, that there are eternal rewards and punishments, and that the virtuous shall receive the one, and the wicked suffer the other; I say, since this is the common faith of Christendom, let us all resolve in the strength of God to live up to what we agree in, before we fall out so miserably about the rest in which we differ. I am persuaded, the change and comfort which that pious course would bring us to, would go very far to dispose our natures to compound easily for all the rest, and we might hope yet to see happy days in poor England; for there I would have so good a work begun. And, how it is possible for the eminent men of every religious persuasion, especially the present ministers of the parishes of England, to think of giving an account to God at the last day, without using the utmost of their endeavours to moderate the members of their respective communions, towards those that differ from them, is a mystery to me. But this I know and must lay it at their doors, I charge also my own soul with it, God requires moderation and humility from us; for he is at hand, who will not spare to judge our impatience, if we have no patience for one another. The eternal God rebuke, I beseech him, the wrath of man, and humble all under the sense of the evil of this day: and yet, unworthy as we are, give us peace, for his holy name's sake.

"It is now time to end this letter, and I will do it without saying any more than this. Thou seest my defence against popular calumny; thou seest what my thoughts are of, our condition, and the way to better it, and thou seest my hearty and humble prayer to Almighty God, to incline us to be wise, if it were but for our own sakes. I shall only add, that I am extremely sensible of the kindness and justice intended me by my friends on this occasion, and that I am for that, and many more reasons,

"Thy obliged and affectionate friend,

"WILLIAM PENN.

"Teddington, October
the 24th, 1688."

Subsequently, he addressed the following epistle to his own religious society, being a clear exposition of the purity of that foundation on which his profession was built, and of his sincerity in upholding it against all the opposition of evilly disposed men: —

"AN EPISTLE GENERAL TO THE PEOPLE OF GOD, CALLED QUAKERS, BY THEIR FRIEND AND BROTHER, WILLIAM PENN.

"Containing, 1st. A testimony to the holy truth and way of God.

"2d. An exhortation to the people of God to walk in it.

"3d. A vindication of himself from the slanders of wicked men.

"Dearly beloved friends and brethren, to whom my soul wisheth the increase of grace, mercy, and peace from God our father and our Lord Jesus Christ:

"It is now about twenty-two years since I embraced the testimony of the blessed truth and the fellowship of it amongst you, which is Christ the light of the world in us, the hope of the glory which is to come. I cannot repine, notwithstanding the many sorts of troubles and afflictions I have met withal on that account, whether they came from my near relations, or the governments of the world, or my neighbours, or my enemies, or my false friends: above all considerations I bow my knee to the God and father of our Lord Jesus Christ, the Lord of Glory, with holy thanks and humble praises, that he has given me the knowledge of himself by the light and grace of his Son in my heart, unto which I turned in my youthful days by that *spiritual* and gospel ministry that God has raised up amongst you, that reached the conscience in word and doctrine. And though I have been compassed about with manifold difficulties in my time and service, yet I can say my desire has been to serve him in the gospel of his Son, for the exaltation of his own glorious name and truth, according to the gift I received from him, from whom every good and perfect gift comes, who is the great *Father of lights and spirits.* By him alone it has been that I have been enabled to speak well of his name from the experience I have had of the goodness he has shown to my soul, both in his judgments and mercies; and I can say that his mercies endure forever; and they that will try, shall find, that *there is mercy with him, that he may be feared.* His word of light, grace, and truth in the heart will cleanse the young man's ways, and guide the old man in the path he should walk, to peace. I found that from the revelation of this word in the soul, springs the true conviction and knowledge of God and a man's self, and by nothing else can man be convicted and born again. Further, I perceived that in this living, revealing word, standeth the true ministry and all acceptable private devotion — religion without this being an empty sound, an insipid thing, an image or picture of a living thing, but it is without real life and motion. To know the convincing, converting, and redeeming power of this word, and to be acquainted with the needful and excellent graces of it — for 'tis a word of faith, reconciliation and patience, meekness and regeneration — I found there must be a sincere retirement of the soul from all self-love, and the lusts and vanities of the world, and an humble and steady waiting for its inward holy monitions and illuminations in the soul, and a resignation to the holy doctrine it teacheth, be it never so cross to our vain desires and carnal inclinations and customs, which unfolded to me the discipline of the *true cross of Christ*, and what it was to take it up daily and follow him that bore it, for the love of him, and that there was no other way to follow Jesus fully, and attain to the glory that shall hereafter be revealed, and that crown which never fades away. Now, friends, here you are, for God has brought you hither to this sense, knowledge, and experience of his new covenant work, which is the glory of the latter days, and though sown in clouds, yet you need not that any one should now teach you, saying, Know the Lord, for I know you know him, and where he dwells, and how to approach him — and therefore here keep, and in the feeling and guidance of this divine word and oracle abide. If any should call upon you, Lo here! and lo there! go not forth, for if it were possible for an angel from heaven to come with another gospel than this word of light and grace in the heart, let him be accursed. Whither should you, or can you go for true satisfaction, when this Word hath the words of eternal life? and it cannot be otherwise, since in this Word is life, and that life is the light of men, and this is the condemnation of the world that it has this light, and yet men will not bring their deeds to it; but the reason is plain, because they love darkness rather than light, and the cause of that is, because their deeds are evil, and will not bear the discovery of that blessed day dawning upon the soul.

"Wherefore, dear friends, that you may be new covenant children, true Jews, circumcision in Spirit, Christians of Christ's christening, and making, by fire and by the Holy Ghost, by the holy water of the word of regeneration, that washes the inside and takes out the spots of the soul, and is called the *laver* of the word; I beseech you in the bowels of Christ Jesus to love this word, and hide it in your hearts, wait upon it and commune with it, that you may know it to be your holy oracle, to inspire, guide, and order you through the whole course of your pilgrimage, till you shall have fought out the good fight of faith, and finished your course, and shall arrive at the rest of God, reserved by him for his people that endure to the end.

"And now, my friends, as concerning the present

ossings and revolutions of things that are in the world, *let your eye be to God; believe not every spirit, nor lay hands suddenly on persons or things*, but be humble and sober, and do to others as you would that they should do to you, and stand still that you may see the salvation of God come in His own way, for so you are to receive it and share in it. And for those *clamours* that have almost darkened the air against *me*, your suffering friend and brother, be neither troubled nor captivated by them, but keep your minds chaste in the dwellings of truth, and possess your souls in patience, and in this true frame of spirit remember me, as I have never forgotten you. But of one thing be assured, *I am innocent* both of the imputation of Jesuitism, Popery, and plots, and my God will in his good time confound their devices that trouble you and me with their false things, though I beseech him to forgive the authors of them as I desire mercy for my own soul. I have *little deserved* this measure and usage from any of the people of this nation. The Lord God Almighty knows I have universally sought the liberty and peace of it, and that nothing may take place to spoil or hinder that good work, nor can any upon earth justly task me with advancing any one thing that unbecomes a Christian and an Englishman; neither blood, Popery, money, nor slavery, can be laid at my door. I wrought as well as I could with the strength and instruments I had, for a general good. If some things were done that were not well done and pleased not, it was no fault of mine, and that is well known to many persons of unquestionable truth.

"*I never accepted of any commission but that of a free and common solicitor for sufferers of all sorts and in all parties,* which made my conversation very general. I thought that charity, which gave me that office, should know no man after the flesh, nor suffer bounds to any that needed it, nor do I find in my conscience that doing what good one can under any government is a sin or a fault, for which a man ought to be stigmatized or evilly entreated. I acknowledge I was an instrument to break the jaws of persecution; to that end I once took the freedom to remember King James of his frequent assurances in favour of liberty of conscience, and with much zeal used my small interest with him to gain that point upon his ministers that he told me were against it. That so the doors of our prisons and meeting-houses, until that time cruelly shut against us, might be opened, and the poor and the widow and the orphan might come forth and praise God in the use of a just freedom. This and personal good offices were my daily business at Whitehall, of which I can take the righteous God of heaven and earth to witness. Nor can I yet see that providence of liberty and peace which we enjoyed under him, was such *a trick or snare* as some have represented it. Harm is to them that harm think; we sought but our just and Christian privilege, and I heartily wish that they that thought so, may do better and answer that great expectation that has been raised in the people's minds about it. One thing I know — could I have apprehended that the good days we had during his reign were a trick to introduce evil ones, all obligations would have ceased with me, and no man more earnestly and cheerfully engaged after my manner against his government than myself. For, alas! what did I seek, or what have I got! What I have spent and lost is much harder to tell. But I leave that with a just and good God to reprize me and mine in his own way and time, as I do to vindicate my opprest innocency against my implacable adversaries, of whom with David I can say, 'they have hated me without a cause,' and as he expresses himself, Psalms 109, v. 1, 2, 3, 4, 5, 'Hold not thy peace, O God of my praise, for the mouth of the wicked and the mouth of the deceitful are opened against me — with a lying tongue have they compassed me about also with words of hatred; and fought against me without a cause; for my love they are my adversaries, but I give myself to prayer; and they have rewarded me evil for good, and hatred for my love.'

"The Lord God Almighty rebuke the wrath and wickedness of man, and look down from heaven upon this broken and sinful nation in his great mercy, and heal it of all its distempers, that we, notwithstanding the judgments of God that seem to gather over our heads as a dark cloud, may yet see righteousness and peace break forth in this land, as the sun in the fulness and strength of his glory. And for you, my dear brethren, in whose cause, and for whose sakes I have been as one killed all the day long, have your conversation, let me entreat you, according to the gospel, in sobriety and humility, in patience and brotherly kindness. Be steadfast and immovable in every good word and work, that in all things you may walk as becometh the true disciples of Christ, whose kingdom is not of this world, and who teacheth his followers how to live in it as they ought to do, rather than how to get it, that so your heavenly Father may be glorified by you, who is worthy, with the Son, to receive all glory and praise, with obedience and reverence, now and for ever.

"I am, in the sufferings and patience of the kingdom of Christ which yet remain, your faithful friend and brother. WILLIAM PENN."

The nation was at this time in a state of general ferment. William, Prince of Orange, was invited to come over, and after landing in Torbay, he and his consort were soon seated on the throne. W. Penn's situation was thus suddenly reversed. He might have retired to the continent, or to Pennsylvania; but, conscious of his own innocence, he resolved not to withdraw, as most of King James's adherents had done, but to remain in England openly as before. In a few weeks, while walking in the garden at Whitehall, he was called before the Lords of the Council, and underwent a close examination; when he declared that he had done, and should do nothing, but what he was willing to answer for before his God and his country. Though no accusation was brought against him, the Council required security for his re-appearance, and then discharged him. At his re-examination, nothing being produced to justify detention, he was liberated in open Court.

In addition to his trials at home, he had others abroad. Matters did not go on well in America: the settlers disagreed and complained without reason; the deputy governor resigned; and, instead of remitting money to the proprietor, they continued to draw on him for more, though he was himself greatly straitened. His letters to the refractory colonists are full of just and generous sentiments.

William Penn soon had the great satisfaction of seeing the Act of Toleration passed in a constitutional manner by the King and Parliament; and though it did not come up to the full extent of his enlarged views, it put a great check on persecution, and was hailed with general approbstion.

In 1690 he was twice arrested. In the first instance he was taken up by some military, in consequence of a letter addressed to him by James, which had been intercepted. On appealing to King William in person, he was brought before him and the Council, and closely examined for two hours, when he made no secret of his attachment to James, but declared that he knew nothing of the letter; that he was sensible of his present duty as a subject; and that he never had the wickedness, even to think of endeavouring to restore to the late King, the crown which had fallen from his head. After giving security for his appearance in Court, he was allowed to withdraw, and on again presenting himself, was honourably discharged a second time. Soon after, King William having gone over to Ireland, and the nation being threatened with an invasion from France, the Queen adopted strong measures, and issued a proclamation for apprehending eighteen persons of importance, considered doubtful, among whom was William Penn. He was committed to prison, but on being brought up before the Court of King's Bench, he was a third time fully acquitted.

For some time he had been making preparations for another voyage to Pennsylvania, where his presence was very necessary, and where he longed for a quiet retreat from secret slander and open outrage. The secretary of state too furthered his intention, and vessels were prepared for him and others. At this time, he attended the funeral of his beloved friend George Fox, and preached to about two thousand persons assembled at the grave. Immediately afterwards, he heard that a fresh charge had been made against him by one Fuller, whom Parliament subsequently pronounced "a notorious impostor and false accuser." He was now convinced that, though innocent, there was no security for him in public; and believing that enmity would supersede justice, he felt justified in seeking retirement, and withdrew to a private lodging in London, where he spent his time in study and religious exercises, with the occasional conversation of a few select friends. His long absence produced serious evils in the province; his own private affairs fell into disorder; the popular clamour against him increased; and, he even fell under the censure of some of his fellow members. To reassure these, he addressed the following short, but touching epistle, to the yearly meeting of 1691, in London.

"The 30th of the Third Month, 1691.

"MY BELOVED, DEAR, AND HONOURED BRETHREN,

"My unchangeable love salutes you; and though I am absent from you, yet I feel the sweet and lowly life of your heavenly fellowship, by which I am with you, and a partaker amongst you, whom I have loved above my chiefest joy. Receive no evil surmisings, neither suffer hard thoughts, through the insinuations of any, to enter your minds against me your afflicted, but not forsaken friend and brother. My enemies are yours, and in the ground, mine for your sakes; and that God seeth in secret, and will one day reward openly. My privacy is not because men have sworn truly, but falsely against me; for wicked men have laid in wait for me, and false witnesses have laid to my charge things that I knew not; who have never sought myself, but the good of all, through great exercises, and have done some good, and would have done more, and hurt to no man, but always desired that truth and righteousness, mercy, and peace might take place amongst us. Feel me near you, and lay me near you, my dear, and beloved brethren, and leave me not, neither forsake, but wrestle with Him that is able to prevail against the cruel desires of some, that we may yet meet in the congregations of his people, as in days past to our mutual comfort. The everlasting God of his chosen in all generations, be in the midst of you, and crown your most solemn assemblies with his blessed presence, that his tender, meek, lowly, and heavenly love and life may flow among you; and that he would please to make it a seasoning and fruitful opportunity to you, that, edified and comforted, you may return home to his glorious high praise, who is worthy for ever. To whom I commit you, desiring to be remembered of you before him, in the nearest and freshest accesses, who cannot forget you in the nearest relation.

"Your faithful friend and brother,

WILLIAM PENN."

John Locke, having come to England with King William, generously desired to return William Penn's former kindness, and offered to procure for him a pardon; but he, sensible of his innocence, and imitating the conduct of his friend, thankfully declined the offer. To add to his other trials, his attached wife was so affected by them that her health gave way; and his many enemies, representing Pennsylvania in a disordered and ruinous state, prevailed on the King in 1692, to deprive him of the government, and confer it on Colonel Fletcher, the Governor of New York. His trials were now at their height; having tasted largely of prosperity, he had to drink as deeply of an adverse cup. But under and through all, divine help sustained his mind, and strengthened him to bear these accumulated afflictions, with humble, but unshaken fortitude, in the consciousness of his own integrity.

To make his retirement profitable to himself and to others, he again employed his pen, and guided by his own extensive and varied experience, wrote an excellent treatise, entitled, "Fruits of Solitude, in Reflections and Maxims, relating to the Conduct of Human Life." Some extracts from the preface, will furnish a good specimen of the value and style of this little work. "The author blesseth God for his retirement, and kisses that gentle hand which led him into it; for, though it should prove barren to the world, it can never do so to him; he has now had some time he could call his own—a property he was never so much master of before; in which he has taken a view of himself and the world, and observed wherein he has hit or missed the mark; what might have been done, what mended, and what avoided in human conduct, together with the omission and excesses of others, as well societies and governments, as private families and persons. And he verily thinks, were he to live over his life again, he could not only, with God's grace, serve him, but his neighbour and himself better than he hath done, and have seven years of his time to spare. And yet, perhaps, he hath not been the worst, or the idlest man in the world, nor is he the oldest. And this is the rather said that it might quicken thee, reader, to lose none of the time that is yet thine."

Another subject which he took up was that of war, then producing great misery; and in "An

Essay toward the present and future peace of Europe," he suggested the idea of a general representative assembly on the continent, for securing peace between the several governments, — an idea which has of later time been repeatedly revived. The seclusion which he observed, does not appear to have been very strict, or to have prevented him from going out occasionally; yet, he was never disturbed; and in 1693, at the end of three years' retirement, Fuller having fallen into deep disgrace, and his accusation not being credited, several noblemen, and others, who were well acquainted with William Penn's character and services, lamenting his hard situation, represented his case to the King. William having a regard for him, readily acceded to their request, that he might enjoy unmolested liberty; and, shortly afterwards, on his appearing before the King and Council, he was honourably acquitted.

His beloved and excellent wife, who had deeply felt the position of his affairs, was now sinking under the effects, and did not survive his enlargement more than a month, when death brought her a peaceful release from anxiety and suffering.

In an affectionate tribute to her worth, William Penn says :—

" During her illness, she uttered many living and weighty expressions, upon divers occasions, both before and near her end. Some of which I took down for mine, and her dear children's consolation.

"At one of the many meetings held in her chamber, we and our children, and one of our servants only being present, in a tendering and living power, she broke out as she sat in her chair, 'Let us all prepare, not knowing what hour or watch the Lord cometh. O, I am full of matter! shall we receive good, and shall we not receive evil things at the hand of the Lord? I have cast my care upon the Lord; he is the physician of value; my expectation is wholly from him. He can raise up, and he can cast down.' A while after she said, 'Oh what shall be done to the unprofitable servant?' At another meeting, before which much heaviness seemed to lie upon her natural spirits, she said, 'This has been a precious opportunity to me; I am finely relieved and comforted, blessed be the Lord.' At another time, as I was speaking to her of the Lord's love, and the witness of his Spirit that was with her, to give her the peace of well doing, she returned to me, looking up, she said, 'I never did, to my knowledge, a wicked thing in all my life.'

"To a friend, aged seventy-five years, that came to see her, she said, 'Thou and I to all appearance are near our ends.' And to another about sixty-five years old, who came also to see her, she said, 'How much older has the Lord made me by this weakness, than thou art! but I am contented, I do not murmur; I submit to his holy will.'

"In the strength of her disease she said, 'It is the great goodness of the Lord, that I should be able to lie thus still. He is the physician of value to me, can I say; let my tongue set forth his praise, and my spirit magnify him whilst I have breath. O, I am ready to be transported beyond my strength. God was not in the thunder, nor in the lightning, but he was heard in the still voice.' She did at several times pray very sweetly, and in all her weakness manifested the most equal, undaunted and resigned spirit, as well as in all other respects. She was an excellent example, both as a child, wife, mother, mistress, friend and neighbour.

"She called the children one day when weak, and said, 'Be not affrighted children, I do not call you to take my leave of you, but to see you, and I would have you walk in the fear of the Lord, and with his people in his holy Truth,' or to that effect.

"Speaking at another time solemnly to the children, she said, 'I never desired any great things for you, but that you may fear the Lord and walk in his Truth, among his people, to the end of your days,' &c.

"She would not suffer me to neglect any public meeting, after I had my liberty, upon her account, saying often, 'O go my dearest! do not hinder any good for me. I desire thee go: I have cast my care upon the Lord: I shall see thee again.'

"About three hours before her end, a relation taking leave of her, she said again, 'I have cast my care upon the Lord. My dear love to all Friends,' and (lifting up her dying hands and eyes) prayed the Lord to preserve them and bless them. About an hour after, causing all to withdraw, we were half an hour together, in which we took our last leave, saying all that was fit upon that solemn occasion. She continued sensible, and did eat something about an hour before her departure; at which time our children, and most of the family were present. She quietly expired in my arms, her head upon my bosom, with a sensible and devout resignation of her soul to Almighty God. I hope, I may say, she was a public, as well as private loss. For, she was not only an excellent wife and mother, but an entire and constant friend, of more than common capacity and great modesty and humility; yet most equal and undaunted in danger. Religious, as well as ingenuous, without affectation. An easy mistress, and good neighbour, especially to the poor. Neither lavish, nor penurious, but an example of industry, as well as of other virtues. Therefore, our great loss is her own eternal gain."

In the mean time, the course of affairs between the Pennsylvanians and the new Governor, was by no means smooth and harmonious. A military, worldly-minded man, he did not either like or understand the views of Friends, who constituted the majority of the colonists, and of the Legislative Assembly. Some of his acts were illegal, and many of them were very unfriendlike. After staying a short time in the province, and confirming the former deputy governor, he retired to his station at New York. The colonists strongly contrasted his conduct with that of William Penn, whom they longed to see amongst them again. His attraction towards them and their country was no less ardent; but he was not then able to gratify his wishes.

He again brought out several short treatises, the chief of which was designed for a preface to the Journal of George Fox, and was entitled "An Account of the Rise and Progress of the People called Quakers." It has been much valued, and often reprinted. The first chapter contains a notice of each distinct body of Christians existing at that time; and some of the views contained in it are very striking.

Two events of a pleasing character soon followed. Many members of his own religious Society, who had disapproved of the active part taken by him in political life, became thoroughly satisfied of his integrity and good motives, and he regained his former place in their Christian regard and affection. In 1694, too, he was restored by the King to the government of Pennsylvania. The language of the instrument reinstating him, was very creditable to William Penn; for, while it pronounced an opinion on the necessity of a small military force on the frontier, it declared, that the disorder and confusion, into which the province and territories had fallen, had been occasioned by his absence; thus, was denied, that which had formed the chief pretence for dispossessing him two years and a half before. A general re-action of feeling in his favour also took place in the public mind in England.

As regards his views on some very important

Christian truths, it may not be unsuitable here to introduce the following quotations from his writings.

From his work, entitled, "A Key to distinguish between the Quaker's religion and the perversions of it." 1692.

"*Perversion* 9. The Quakers deny the Trinity. Nothing less; they believe in the Holy Three, or Trinity of Father, Word, and Spirit, according to Scripture. And, that these Three are truly and properly one; of one nature as well as will. But they are very tender of quitting Scripture terms and phrases for schoolmen's; such as distinct and separate persons and subsistences, &c., from whence people are apt to entertain gross ideas and notions."

"*Perversion* 10. The Quakers deny Christ to be God. A most untrue and unreasonable censure," &c.

"*Perversion* 11. They deny the human nature of Christ. We never taught, said, or held so gross a thing, if by human nature be understood the manhood of Christ Jesus. For, as we believe him to be God over all blessed for ever, so we do, as truly believe him, to be of the seed of David and Abraham, according to the flesh, and, therefore, truly and properly man," &c.

In his work, entitled, "Primitive Christianity Revived," he says, "We do believe, that Jesus Christ was our holy sacrifice, atonement, and propitiation; that he bore our iniquities, and that, by his stripes, we were healed of the wounds Adam gave us in his fall; and that God is just in forgiving true penitents upon the credit of that holy offering Christ made of himself to God for us; and that, what he did and suffered, satisfied and pleased God, and was for the sake of fallen man, that had displeased God; and that, through the offering up of himself once for all, through the Eternal Spirit, he hath for ever perfected those, in all times, that were sanctified, who walked not after the flesh, but after the Spirit."—Rom. viii. 1.

In a tract, entitled, "A Serious Apology for the Principles and Practices of the people called Quakers," written by William Penn, during a confinement in Newgate, to which prison he had been committed for six months, for no other cause than preaching the gospel to his brethren, at one of their meetings, and refusing to disobey the commandments of Christ, by taking an oath, he says in the sixth chapter, "I am constrained for the sake of the simple-hearted, to publish to the world, of our faith in God, Christ, and the Holy Spirit." "We do believe in one only, holy God Almighty, who is an eternal Spirit, the Creator of all things."

"And in one Lord Jesus Christ, his only Son, and express image of his substance, who took upon him flesh, and was in the world; and in life, doctrine, miracles, death, resurrection, ascension, and mediation, perfectly did, and does continue to do, the will of God; to whose holy life, power, mediation, and blood, we only ascribe our sanctification, justification, redemption, and perfect salvation."

"And we believe in one Holy Spirit, that proceeds and breathes from the Father and the Son, a measure of which is given to all to profit with; and he that has one, has all; for those Three are One, who is the Alpha and Omega, the First and the Last, God over all, blessed for ever, Amen."

## CHAPTER VII. 1695-1718.

MARRIES H. CALLOWHILL—ACCOUNT OF SPRINGETT PENN—INTERVIEWS WITH THE CZAR—REVISITS PENNSYLVANIA—PENNSBURY MANOR—INTERESTING INCIDENTS—OPPOSES SLAVE TRADE—THE COLONY PEACEABLE AND PROSPEROUS—FOUNDING OF PUBLIC SCHOOL—HIS PECUNIARY DIFFICULTIES—INGRATITUDE OF OTHERS—WITHDRAWS FOR A YEAR—MORTGAGES, AND OFFERS TO SELL, HIS PROVINCE—HIS HEALTH DECLINES—LONG FEEBLE STATE—DEATH, BURIAL, AND CHARACTER.

We next find William Penn travelling as a minister into the west of England, and holding crowded religious meetings at Bristol, Wells, and other places; then petitioning Parliament to make the affirmation of Friends equivalent to an oath; and further prosecuting this object by attending the House of Commons on their behalf.

In 1696, he married Hannah Callowhill, of Bristol, and soon after removed to that city. His wife was pious and judicious, and the connection contributed greatly to his comfort and advantage; but a severe trial soon followed, in the death of his eldest son, Springett Penn, a religious and very promising young man, then in his twenty-first year, of whose striking expressions and conduct in his last illness, the father has left the following, touching account:—

"My very dear child and eldest son, Springett Penn, from his childhood, manifested a disposition to goodness, and gave me hope of a more than ordinary capacity; and time satisfied me in both respects. Besides a good share of learning, and especially of mathematical knowledge, he showed a judgment in the use and application of it, much above his years. He had the seeds of many good qualities rising in him, which made him beloved, and consequently lamented; but, especially his humility, plainness, and truth; with a tenderness and softness of nature, that if I may say it, were an improvement upon his other good qualities. And, though these were no security against sickness and death, yet they went a good way to facilitate a due preparation for them. Indeed, the good ground that was in him, showed itself very plainly sometime before his illness. For more than half a year before it pleased the Lord to visit him with weakness, he grew more retired, and much disengaged from youthful delights; showing a remarkable tenderness in meetings, even when they were silent. But, when he saw himself doubtful as to his recovery, he turned his mind and meditations more apparently towards the Lord; secretly, as also when those were in the room who attended upon him, praying often with great fervency to the Lord, and uttering many thankful expressions and praises to Him, in a very deep and sensible manner. One day he said to us, 'I am resigned to what God pleaseth; he knows what is best. I would live if it pleased him that I might serve him. But, O Lord, not my will, but thy will be done.'

"One speaking to him of the things of this world,

and what might please him when recovered; he answered, 'My eye looks another way, where the truest pleasure is.' When he told me he had rested well, and I said it was a mercy to him, he quickly replied upon me, with a serious, yet sweet look, 'All is mercy, dear father, every thing is mercy.' Another time, when I went to meeting, at parting, he said, 'Remember me, my dear father, before the Lord. Though I cannot go to meetings, yet I have many good meetings; the Lord comes in upon my spirit; I have heavenly meetings with him by myself.'

"Not many days before he died, while alone, the Lord appeared by his holy power upon his spirit, and at my return, asking him how he did, he told me, 'O, I have had a sweet time, a blessed time! Great enjoyments. The power of the Lord overcame my soul: a sweet time, indeed!'

"On my telling him how some of the gentry who had been to visit him, were gone to their games, and sports and pleasures, and how little consideration the children of men had of God and their latter end; and how much happier he was in this weakness, to have been otherwise educated, and to be preserved from those temptations to vanity, &c., he answered, 'It is all stuff, my dear father: it is sad stuff. O that I might live to tell them so!' 'Well, my dear child,' I replied, 'let this be the time of thy entering into secret covenant with God, that if he raise thee, thou wilt dedicate thy youth, strength, and life to him, and his people and service.' He returned,

'Father, that is not now to do; it is not now to do;' with great tenderness upon his spirit.

"Being almost ever near him, and doing any thing for him he wanted or desired, he broke out with much sense and love, 'My dear father, if I live, I will make thee amends.' And speaking to him of Divine enjoyments, that the eye of man saw not, but the soul, made alive by the spirit of Christ, plainly felt; he, in a lively remembrance, cried out, 'I had a sweet time yesterday by myself! the Lord hath preserved me to this day! O blessed be his name; my soul praises him for his mercy! Father, it is of the goodness of the Lord, that I am as well as I am!' Fixing his eyes upon his sister, he took her by the hand, saying, 'Poor Tishe, look to good things; poor child, there is no comfort without it. One drop of the love of God is worth more than all the world. I know it; I have tasted it: I have felt as much, or more of the love of God in this weakness, than in all my life before.' At another time, as I stood by him, he looked up upon me, and said, 'Dear father, sit by me, I love thy company, and I know thou lovest mine; and if it be the Lord's will that we must part, be not troubled, for that will trouble me.'

"Taking something one night in bed, just before going to rest, he sat up, and fervently prayed thus: 'O Lord God, thou whose Son said to his disciples, Whatsoever ye ask in my name, ye shall receive; I pray thee, in His name, bless this to me this night, and give me rest, if it be thy blessed will, O Lord!' And, accordingly he had a very comfortable night, of which he took a thankful notice before us next day.

"And when he, at one time, more than ordinarily, expressed a desire to live, and entreated me to pray for him; he added, 'dear father, if the Lord should raise me and enable me to serve him and his people, then I might travel with thee sometimes, and we might ease one another (meaning in the ministry): he spoke it with great modesty.' Upon which I said to him, 'my dear child, if it please the Lord to raise thee, I am satisfied it will be so; and if not, then inasmuch as it is thy fervent desire in the Lord, he will look upon thee just as if thou didst live to serve him, and thy comfort will be the same: so either way it will be well. For, if thou shouldst not live, I do verily believe thou wilt have the recompense of thy good desires, without the temptations and troubles that would attend, if long life were granted to thee.'

"Saying, one day, 'I am resolved I will have such a thing done;' he immediately catched himself, and fell into this reflection, with much contrition, 'Did I say, I will? O Lord, forgive me that irreverent and hasty expression! I am a poor, weak creature, and live by thee, and, therefore, I should have said, 'If it pleaseth thee that I live, I intend to do so, or so;' Lord forgive my rash expression.'

"Seeing my present wife ready to be helpful, and do any thing for him, he turned to her, and said, 'Don't thou do so, let them; don't trouble thyself so much for such a poor creature as I am.' On her taking leave of him a few nights before his end, he said to her, 'Pray for me, dear mother: thou art good and innocent, it may be the Lord may hear thy prayers for me, for I desire my strength again, that I might live, and employ it more in the Lord's service.'

"Two or three days before his departure, he called his brother to him, and looking awfully upon him, said, 'Be a good boy, and know there is a God, a great and mighty God, who is a rewarder of the righteous, and so is he of the wicked, but their rewards are not the same. Have a care of idle people and idle company, and love good company and good Friends, and the Lord will bless thee: I have seen good things for thee since my sickness, if thou dost but fear the Lord. And, if I should not live, though the Lord is all sufficient, remember what I say to thee, when I am dead and gone: poor child, the Lord bless thee, come and kiss me!' Which melted us all into great tenderness, but his brother more particularly.

"Many good exhortations he gave to some of the servants, and others who came to see him, that were not of our communion, as well as those that were, which drew tears from their eyes.

"The day but one before he died, he went to take the air in a coach; but said, at his return, 'Really, father, I am exceedingly weak, thou canst not think how weak I am.' 'My dear child,' I replied, 'thou art weak, but God is strong, who is the strength of thy life:' 'Ay, that is it,' said he, 'which upholdeth me.' The day before he departed, being alone with him, he desired me to fasten the door; and looking earnestly upon me, said, 'Dear father, thou art a dear father, and I know thy Father, come let us two have a little meeting, a private ejaculation together, now no body else is here. O my soul is sensible of the love of God!' And indeed a sweet time we had, like to precious ointment for his burial.

"He desired to go home, if not to live, to die there, and we made preparation for it, being twenty miles from my house; and so much stronger was his spirit than his body, that he spoke of going next day, which was the morning he departed; and a symptom it was of his great journey to his longer home. That morning he left us, growing more and more sensible of his extreme weakness, he asked me, as doubtful of himself, 'How shall I go home?' I told him in a coach; he answered, 'I am best in a coach.' But observing his decay, I said, 'Why child? thou art at home everywhere;' 'Ay,' said he, 'so I am in the Lord.' I took that opportunity to ask him if I should remember his love to his friends at Bristol, London, &c. 'Yes, yes,' said he, 'my love in the Lord; my love to all Friends in the Lord:' 'And relations too?' he said, 'Ay, to be sure.' Being asked if he would have his ass' milk, or eat any thing; he answered, 'No more outward food, but heavenly food is provided for me.'

"His time drawing on apace, he said to me, 'My dear father, kiss me, thou art a dear father, I desire to prize it: how can I make thee amends?'

"He also called his sister, and said to her, 'Poor

child, come and kiss me:' there seemed a tender and long farewell between them. I sent for his brother that he might kiss him too, which he did: all were in tears about him, and turning his head to me, he said, softly, 'Dear father, hast thou no hope for me?' I answered, 'My dear child, I am afraid to hope, and I dare not despair; but am, and have been resigned, though one of the hardest lessons I ever learned.' He paused awhile, and with a composed frame of mind, said, 'Come life, come death, I am resigned: O the love of God overcomes my soul!' Feeling himself decline apace, and seeing him not able to bring up the matter that was in his throat, somebody fetched the doctor, but so soon as he came in, he said, 'Let my father speak to the doctor, and I will go to sleep; which he did, and waked no more;' breathing his last on my breast, the 10th day of the second month, between the hours of nine and ten in the morning, 1696, in his one and twentieth year.

"So ended the life of my dear child and eldest son, much of my comfort and hope, and one of the most tender and dutiful, as well as ingenuous and virtuous youths, I knew, if I may say so of my own dear child. In him I lost all that any father can lose in a child, since he was capable of any thing that became a sober young man; my friend and companion, as well as most affectionate and dutiful child.

"May this loss and end have its due weight and impression upon all his dear relations and friends, and those to whose hands this account may come, for their remembrance and preparation for their great and last change; and I shall have my end in making my dear child thus far public.

"WILLIAM PENN."

The Czar of Russia, afterwards called Peter the Great, having come to England to obtain useful knowledge of various kinds, William Penn and other Friends had interesting interviews with him; with which the Czar evinced his satisfaction not only by his remarks, but by frequently attending the meetings for worship at Deptford and other places, and by marked attention, as occasions offered, to members of the Society. With two other Friends William Penn next paid a visit to Ireland, where he had a considerable estate requiring his superintendence; he also felt it his duty to labour in the spiritual vineyard of that island. Large meetings were held, in which he preached the truths of the gospel, many persons of distinction attending them. An interview with the bishop of Cork was satisfactory; but, subsequent alarm at the crowded meetings, induced the bishop to resort to magisterial authority, and to employ his own pen, to counteract the influence of the doctrines preached.

At length, after an absence of fifteen years, and many yearnings towards his friends in Pennsylvania, William Penn revisited the province in 1699, taking his wife and family with him. On this occasion, he again wrote an excellent address to his children on their civil and religious conduct, as well as an instructive farewell epistle to his friends, who gave him certificates of their esteem and full unity. The voyagers embarked at Cowes, and after a tedious passage of nearly three months, arrived safely at Philadelphia, at a time when a malignant fever was prevailing in the country. The people welcomed him with marks of universal joy, hoping that he was come to spend the remainder of his days among them. The assembly soon met, and William Penn occupied his time, not only in his duties as governor, but in those of a gospel minister.

His was a rare instance of Christian legislation. Liberty of conscience was a chief corner-stone of the political edifice in his infant republic; the reformation of the offender became the first object of his criminal code. He united in himself two characters as a principal person in a visible Church, and as head of a state. Had an attempt, however, been made to transmit the union, after the manner of Europe, to succeeding generations, its utter failure would have soon become apparent; for his eldest surviving son, so far from inheriting his religious character, caused him, in after years, much grief, by his gross misconduct and vicious excesses.

A writer* of our own day, says, in allusion to the character of William Penn, "We should remember that the present times are profiting by the exertions of those generous spirits, for, in the progress of human affairs, mankind build in every subsequent age, on foundations formerly laid. What veneration

* Deborah Logan.

and respect must we acknowledge to be due to the man who, living at a period when the principles of civil and religious liberty had to contend for their existence, with a base and sordid despotism, voluntarily stepped forth as their champion, and triumphantly rescued, and handed down to us some of the proudest distinctions of his country. A man who spent his whole life, and all the means which he possessed, in endeavouring to benefit mankind, and, finally, by exhibiting to the world a scheme of government, founded on the benevolent principles of Christianity, and which were administered by himself in the same spirit, has shown by the unexampled prosperity and success which has attended it, how consonant such principles are with the true interests of society. Is not a character, that effected such noble purposes, entitled to the gratitude and esteem of the latest posterity?"

The Governor and his family took up their residence at his mansion of Pennsbury.

This manor was situated in Bucks Co., about twenty-four miles above Philadelphia, on the river Delaware. It comprised upwards of 6000 acres of fertile soil, mostly covered with majestic forests. While in the possession of an Indian king, it had borne the name of Sepassin.

The mansion was built in 1682–3, and was about sixty feet front, facing the river. It was two stories high, and of brick. On the first floor was a large hall, used on public occasions for the meetings of the council, and the entertainment of strangers and the

Indians A broad walk through an avenue of poplars led to the river. The house was surrounded by gardens and lawns, and the more distant woods were opened in vistas, looking down the Delaware, and upwards towards the Falls of Trenton.

These woods had been laid out in walks at the proprietary's first visit, and the preservation of the trees are enjoined in several of his letters. He sent out from England, walnuts, hawthorns, hazels, fruit trees, and a great variety of the rarest seeds and roots. While in this country he procured from Maryland several panniers of trees and shrubs, indigenous in that province, and directed that the most beautiful wild flowers should be transplanted into his gardens.

On the whole, his instructions indicate a love of nature, and an elegance of taste, which are very remarkable. Tradition relates, that on one occasion, when he made a feast for his red brethren, a long table was spread for them in the avenue leading from the house, which was shaded by poplars; and among the viands provided were one hundred turkeys, besides venison and other meats.

The proprietor frequently visited on horseback the meetings of Friends, in Pennsylvania and New Jersey. On one of these visits, when going to Haverford, it is related, "that he overtook a little girl named Rebecca Wood, who was going afoot from Darby to attend the same meeting. On coming up with her, he enquired where she was going, and being informed, he with his usual good nature desired her to get up behind him, and bringing his horse to a convenient place she mounted, and so rode away on the bare back."

This incident affords a pleasing evidence of that kindness and condescension, which the governor manifested towards all classes of society.

Tradition also informs us "that when he was visiting meetings in Pennsylvania, he lodged one night at Merion, where a boy about twelve years old, son of the person at whose house he lodged, being a lad of curiosity, and not often seeing such great men, privately crept to the chamber, up a flight of steps on the outside of the building. On peeping through the latchet hole, he was struck with awe in beholding this great man on his knees by the bed-side, and in hearing what he said; for, he could distinctly hear him in prayer and thanksgiving, that he was then provided for in the wilderness."

Among the various objects to which his attention was zealously directed, were the instruction and civilization of the Indian tribes, and the improvement of the condition of the African slaves; for it was not in his power to prevent their being brought into the colony. The Friends there had already, at their Yearly Meetings in 1688 and 1696, declared the buying, selling, and holding of men in slavery, to be inconsistent with the Christian religion. This entirely agreed with the sentiments of the Governor and Council, but not with those of the Assembly; which, being composed of men of various characters, negatived his measures for elevating the slaves' condition. They concluded, after much demur, to raise the sum of two thousand pounds a year, for the expenses of the government.

He spent about two years among his people, applying himself diligently to his various duties, "preferring the good of the country and its inhabitants to his own private interests; rather remitting than rigorously exacting his lawful revenues; so that, under the influence of his paternal administration, he left the province in an easy and a flourishing condition."

The important subject of education had early claimed the care of William Penn, and of the Friends who had emigrated to Pennsylvania. A school was set up, in the privileges of which the poor, as well as the rich, were to participate. Perceiving the necessity of establishing this on an enlarged and permanent basis, a charter was granted by the proprietary in 1701, which was confirmed with some alterations and enlargement of powers, by two subsequent charters in 1708 and 1711.

An extract from the preamble of the last charter will show the liberal views of the founders of the school: "Whereas, the prosperity and welfare of any people depend in a great measure upon the good education of youth, and their early instruction in the principles of religion and virtue, and qualifying them to serve their country and themselves by breeding them in reading, writing, and learning of languages, and useful arts and sciences, suitable to their age, sex, and degree, which cannot be effected in any manner so well as by erecting public schools for the purposes aforesaid; and, whereas, &c."

William Penn directed that the seal of this corporation * should have for its inscription, "Good Instruction is better than Riches."

Under the charter several schools were subsequently established, in which the course of instruction was liberal and comprehensive. A classical school was carefully maintained under some of the best teachers of their time, and a vigilant supervision was exercised by those Friends who were chosen overseers.

By a reference to the minutes of the corporation some years later, we find that instructions were given to the teachers, "that the foremost of the pupils should be required to give in writing the most elegant translations of the Latin authors they have read, whether prose or verse, that their capacity will allow; as by this practice they will more strongly impress upon their memories the language and subjects they are reading, improve their handwriting, style, and spelling, learn readily to write their native language correctly and with elegance, invite them to read history in English, give them a relish for the best English authors, and induce them to an imitation of their style and sentiments, when they come to be exercised in composing English

* This corporate body still continues in Philadelphia, and has under its care nine good schools, in which, without any sectarian preferences, the poor of the city are taught gratis, and those who are able to pay, at reasonable rates.

themes, or upon any occasion in public or private life."

While the founders of the religious society of Friends fully recognized the importance of all useful and liberal learning, to prepare their youth for the performance of their duties, as good citizens of the community in which they might live, they were at the same time fully aware of the primary necessity of training their youth in true religion, and in the fear of God. On this subject, George Fox says, in a letter addressed to the Society in 1683, "It is desired that all Friends that have children, families, and servants, may train them up in the pure and unspotted religion, and in the nurture and fear of God, and that frequently they read the Holy Scriptures. And exhort and admonish them that every family apart, may serve and worship the Lord, as well as in public." In unison with this, we have also a treatise of William Penn, entitled: —

"*Christian Discipline, or certain good and wholesome Orders, for the well governing of my family in a right Christian conversation, as becometh the Children of the Light and Truth of the most High God. Divided into Two Parts. By William Penn.*"

From which the following extract is taken :—

"'Now, therefore, fear the Lord, and serve him in sincerity and in truth; and put away the gods which your fathers served beyond the flood and in Egypt, and serve the Lord: and if it seem evil unto you to serve the Lord, choose you this day whom ye will serve; whether the gods which your fathers served (that were beyond the flood) or the gods of the Amorites, in whose land ye dwell; but, as for me and my house, we will serve the Lord.'"—JOSH. xxiv. 14, 15.

"1.—As it becometh us, to whom is made known the only wise, invisible, and omnipotent God, and that heavenly, spiritual worship, which only pleaseth Him,—always to retain Him in our knowledge with all due fear, godly reverence and sincere obedience; so more especially it is my appointment in the heavenly authority, as a Christian master of my family, that all in it, and of it, who profess the Truth with me, do meet and assemble every morning, with all humility and godly fear, to wait upon the Almighty God or Creator, and to receive and enjoy his living mercies and refreshing presence; that, being sanctified by Him, we may hallow His name, and return the praise which is due to him from men and angels for ever.

"2.—That every day about the eleventh hour, (unless diverted by extraordinary occasions, which is also intended and excepted of every time herein appointed), all come together again; and every one in his turn, read either the Scriptures of Truth, or some martyrology.

"3.—That the same practice be observed about the sixth hour in the evening; to the end, that we may be stirred up to abhor the actions of evil doers, and to embrace and follow the example of patience, zeal, holiness, and constancy in the righteous, who only were and are of the flock and family of God.

"4. — That those days which are appointed to meet publicly to worship God upon, none on any pretence (being in health, and not unavoidably engaged to the contrary) neglect going to such meetings; — but that they constantly and timely attend and frequent the same, as becometh a family fearing the Lord, and that is zealous for his living Truth.

"5. — That there be a watch kept over every mind, so as that it may not err from the counsel of God, and the weighty government of his holy truth, in whatsoever it is exercised about; lest darkness and deadness come over it, and the evil one enter, to sow all manner of evil seeds, as strife, envy, evil watchings, levity, pride, and such like: the latter end of such is worse than their beginning."

Taking leave of the colonists and the Indians, William Penn embarked for England in the autumn of 1701, and after a voyage of six weeks landed at Portsmouth.

On Queen Anne's accession to the throne, he occasionally attended her Court, the Queen being favourable to him, and interested by his conversation on American affairs. His return home had been hastened by a report that the colonies were to be transferred to the royal government; but this was soon dispelled. His accounts from Pennsylvania were, however, painful. The Assembly showed their contumacy even more than before, and disagreed with the local government; refusing the supplies which were really due and necessary to the Governor in return for his generosity, and for large outlays which he could ill afford.

As long as William Penn lived, and for the greater part of a century from the first foundation of the colony, the government was conducted in its various departments without administering an oath; the constable's staff was the only instrument of authority, and soldiers were not employed in the province; while all the religious bodies dwelt together on equal terms. What an example is here afforded to European states!

William Penn again visited as a minister some of the western counties of England, where his religious services were effectual to the spiritual advancement of some, and to the restoration of others. His pen also was often employed in the cause of truth and righteousness. His trials in pecuniary matters however increased, and greatly embittered his declining years. To various persons he had behaved with great generosity, but it was in many instances ill-requited; his remittances from the colony, on which he had expended twenty thousand pounds, and where private wealth was rapidly accumulating, were very scanty and much in arrear, though he earnestly intreated punctual payment to meet his own requirements. In fact, he seems to have supported the government, instead of being supported by it. His extensive undertakings and wide spread liberality had exceeded his means. An unsuspecting disposition had also laid him open to fraud. The executors of Ford, his steward, in whom he had placed implicit, but mistaken confidence, made heavy and very unjust demands upon him; an expensive lawsuit, and an appeal to the Court of Chancery followed; and, at length, obtaining no redress, in order to avoid the enforcement of those demands, he was under the painful necessity of again secluding himself, and living for about a year within the rules of the Fleet. From this he was relieved only by mortgaging his province to some of his friends for six thousand six hundred pounds.

"Throughout the whole of this vexatious and humiliating business, he exercised the patience and fortitude of the true Christian, whose affections are fixed not on earthly but on heavenly things, and the beautiful remark of Isaac Norris, seemed applicable to him, "God darkens this world to us, that our eyes may behold the greater brightness of his kingdom."*

His health now began to fail; yet he still went occasionally to Whitehall, and continued some of his active pursuits. He had latterly resided at or near Kensington; he now retired to Ruscombe, in Berkshire. In 1711 he published his last production; which, though only a preface to the writings of his friend John Banks, and dictated as he walked up and down the room with a cane in his hand, carries its own evidence as the production of a master mind,

*Janney's Life of Penn.

rich in intelligence and Christian experience. In the next year, the Assembly of Pennsylvania passed an Act to prevent the importation of negroes, but the home government annulled the measure. He now concluded to sell his province to the Queen, and twelve thousand pounds was the price agreed on; but, before the transfer could be made, he had several paralytic seizures, which prevented it from being completed.

For some years he remained in a very feeble state of body and mind, yet full of childlike innocence and love, often attending his own meeting, and sometimes ministering in it "with the spirit, and with the understanding also."

About this time Thomas Story visited him, and says, "When I went to his house I thought myself strong enough to see him in that condition; but when I entered the room and perceived the great defect of his expression for want of memory, it greatly bowed my spirit under a consideration of the uncertainty of all human qualifications; and what the finest of men are soon reduced to by a disorder of the organs of that body, with which the soul is connected and acts during this present state of being. When these are a little obstructed in their various functions, a man of the clearest parts, and finest expression, becomes scarcely intelligible. Nevertheless, no insanity or lunacy at all appeared in his actions, and his mind was in an innocent state, as appeared by his very loving deportment to all that came near him. And that he had a good sense of truth was plain by some very clear sentences he spoke in the life and power of truth, in an evening meeting we had there; wherein, we were greatly comforted, so that I was ready to think this was a sort of sequestration of him from all the concerns of this life, which so much oppressed him; not in judgment, but in mercy, that he might not be oppressed thereby to the end."

To some friends, who had paid him a visit and were about to leave, he said, "My love is with you, the Lord preserve you and remember me, in the everlasting covenant." His faithful wife was his judicious helper and affectionate attendant. In the year 1718, he peacefully closed his interesting, honourable, and laborious life, in the seventy-fourth year of his age.

In the testimony concerning William Penn, issued by the Monthly Meeting of Friends, for Berkshire, England, a few months after his decease, is the following tribute to his character.

"Being a member of our monthly meeting at the time of his decease, and for some years before, we can do no less than say something of the character of so worthy a man; and not only refer to other meetings, where his residence was in former times, who are witnesses of the great self-denial he underwent in the prime of his youth, and the patience with which he bore many a heavy cross; but, think it our duty to cast in our mite, to set forth in part his deserved commendation."

"He was a man of great abilities, of an excellent

sweetness of disposition; quick of thought and of ready utterance; full of the qualifications of true discipleship, even love without dissimulation; as extensive in charity as comprehensive in knowledge, and to whom malice and ingratitude were utter strangers —ready to forgive enemies, and the ungrateful were not excepted."

Had not the management of his temporal affairs been attended with some deficiencies, envy itself would be, to seek for matter of accusation; and, judging in charity, even that part of his conduct may be attributed to a peculiar sublimity of mind, notwithstanding which he may without straining his character be ranked among the learned, good and great; whose abilities are sufficiently manifested throughout his elaborate writings, which are so many lasting monuments of his admired qualifications, and are the esteem of learned and judicious men among all persuasions.

"And, although in old age, by reason of some shocks of a violent disease, his intellect was much impaired, yet his sweetness and loving disposition surmounted its utmost efforts, and remained when reason almost failed.

"In fine, he was learned without vanity; apt without forwardness; facetious in conversation, yet weighty and serious; of an extraordinary greatness of mind, yet void of the stain of ambition; as free from rigid gravity as he was clear of unseemly levity; a man—a scholar—a friend; whose memorial will be valued by the wise, and blessed with the just."

"A TESTIMONY OF FRIENDS IN PENNSYLVANIA, CONCERNING THEIR DECEASED FRIEND AND GOVERNOR, WILLIAM PENN.

"We find ourselves under obligation and concern, both in duty and affection, to give this mark of our love, and the honourable regard we bear to the memory of our late worthy Governor, and well-beloved friend William Penn; though it may not be our part to attempt so ample and general a testimony as seems justly called for, by his early convincement of the blessed Truth, his noble resignation thereunto, his steadfastness therein, and great services to the Church of Christ; as well by incessant labours in word and doctrine, (made more extensive by the many excellent writings he hath published), as his valiant sufferings for purity of worship, and the testimonies he had received, which to him might be the greater trial and conflict, his birth and station in the world placing him more in the notice of those of high rank amongst men, than was commonly the lot of many others of our worthy elders. Neither can it, we presume, be forgotten, how, when it pleased the Lord to give some ease to his people, this our dear friend employed the interest he then had with success, and devoted his time and purse to serve, not only his friends in their religious liberties, but them and others distressed, or any wanting favour, even to the neglect of his own just interest But these memorials we leave to be made by those of our worthy elders in Great Britain, who have more instances and greater knowledge of those his trials, services, and labours, than many of us can be presumed to be so fully acquainted with.

"Yet it becomes us particularly to say, that as he was our Governor, he merited from us love, and true honour, and we cannot but have the same regard to his memory, when we consider the blessings and ease we have enjoyed under his government; and are rightly sensible of his care, affection, and regard, always shown with anxious concern for the safety and prosperity of the people, who, many of them, removed from comfortable livings to be adventurers with him—not so much with views of better acquisitions, or greater riches, but the laudable prospect of retired, quiet habitations for themselves and posterity, and the promotion of truth and virtue in the earth. And, as his love was great and endeavours constant for the happiness of his friends, countrymen, and fellow-subjects, so was his great tenderness, justice, and love towards the Indians, from first to last, always conspicuous and remarkable. Here we cannot but gratefully and humbly acknowledge to the gracious God of all our mercies, the wonderful preservation of this colony from such injuries and barbarous depredations as have befallen most others; and add that we believe the same love wherewith the Lord had so fully and effectually prevailed on the heart of this our worthy friend, was the chief and durable motive of his affection and kind behaviour towards those people; and was the cause, as he was made a means, of this our peace and preservation; so that his name remains precious, even amongst the heathens.

"More might be truly said of him as he was the proprietary and governor of this province; and we now find it our duty, (incited thereto by the love of our Heavenly Father in our souls) to add a few lines concerning him, as he was our worthy elder, friend, and brother in the blessed Truth; many of us having been often comforted, edified, and solaced with him in the enjoyment thereof. As was his testimony, so was his conversation,—edifying and lovely, administering grace and knowledge. His behaviour was sweet and engaging, and his condescension great, even to the weakest and meanest; affable and of easy access; tender of every person and thing that had simplicity of truth, or honesty for a foundation.

"It was our comfort to understand, that after all his various troubles, trials, and afflictions, when, in an advanced age, infirmity of body, and a distemper which affected his memory in most other things which befell him, yet the love of God remained with him, and his sense thereof was frequently strong and evident, and, we doubt not, the blessing of the Almighty was his Omega.

"So that we have assured hope, those afflictions being put off with his mortal body, immortality is given him by our Lord Jesus, and, as he faithfully bore the cross, the crown, which was his hope, and long since in his eye, is his possession; and his soul received into that bliss prepared and appointed for the righteous.

"Signed at the time of our General Meeting, held in Philadelphia, the 16th of first month, 1718–19."

The last decline, and death and burial of this venerable man are thus pathetically described* by H. Colquhoun, a modern writer, who has shown a greater desire than some others to do justice to his memory. "Gently did the Master whom he had served guide his sinking servant through five years of decay—so gently that the children who loved, and the friends who tended him, watched with chastened sorrow, not unmixed with pleasure, the moral radiance, which, in life's sunset, lingered round the mental ruin. In 1718 came release. [At Jordans] in a quiet hamlet of Buckinghamshire, by the side of his first and much loved wife, and of the son whom he had lost, the great philanthropist was laid to rest; among a concourse, not of Quakers only and neighbours, but of men from all parts of England, drawn together by the fame of so many virtues, and the wish to do them homage. A few words were spoken by those who knew him, to the throng who had heard of his merits; and they laid him in the grave, which closed over great services, and an illustrious name. No stone was set to mark the spot; but the name and services of Penn are written, in the durable monument of religious toleration which he secured, in the unwearying integrity which he practised, and in the institutions of one of those great states in the western world, which now exercise so wide an influence over the destiny of mankind."

* "Short Sketches of some notable Lives."

## CHAPTER VIII.

### THE CALUMNIOUS CHARGES OF MACAULAY AGAINST PENN.

In a former chapter, allusion was made to false charges, which, in our own time, have been made against William Penn. So often has it been the lot of good men to be misrepresented, and yet, so generally does history vindicate sooner or later the great benefactors of the race, that these accusations might, perhaps, be safely left to be refuted by the admitted facts of Penn's eventful life, or by his undeniable characteristics. They form, however, a feature, in what claims to be a model of historical composition, and is unquestionably a work of genius. The vast circulation of Macaulay's volumes, must bring his statements under the notice of many who may have little opportunity to test their truth; his unscrupulous persistence in calumny will have weight with some; while, in all ages, there are unhappily those who, weary of hearing the praise of good men, would gladly excuse their own faults by dwelling on the imputed errors of the great teachers of mankind. It seems, therefore, desirable, as briefly as possible, to review the efforts made by Macaulay to destroy the well earned reputation of William Penn.

Passing by vague and general assertions, which are not attempted to be proven, it is proposed to notice the specific charges in the order in which they occur.

The first is the statement in reference to the fines imposed on the school girls at Taunton, who, under the direction of their teacher, and unconscious of crime, presented a standard to the Duke of Monmouth during his rebellion. The maids of honour to the Queen, having, in accordance with a barbarous usage of that court, obtained an interest in the fines to be wrung from these poor children, employed an agent to make the most profitable composition with their parents. Macaulay affirms positively, that William Penn accepted this agency, and proceeds to assign imaginary excuses, which he may have made to himself for so shameful a course. The only evidence which he adduces to prove his assertion, is a letter from the Secretary of State, addressed to "Mr. Penne," stating the wish of the maids of honour to employ him for this purpose. There is not one word of testimony to show that William Penn accepted this agency; it is not known that any one except Macaulay ever charged him with having had any part in the business—and, there is no good reason to suppose, that he was ever asked to take such part. There was then living a certain George Penne, whose character fitted him for such employment, who was notoriously engaged as a "pardon broker," and who was no doubt the person addressed by Sunderland—his name was spelt as in the letter, with the final "e." William's Penn's name, well-known to the Secretary, and familiar through his father, the Admiral, to all persons in official station, was not so spelt. A cotemporary historian, Oldmixon, who lived within a few miles of Taunton, speaks of some of the circumstances as having been within his own knowledge, and mentions expressly the names of the agent, and the sub-agent employed in this business, the former a popish lawyer, and the latter a resident of the town, in which the narrator lived. Macaulay quotes Oldmixon as authority for a part of the story, but conceals the fact that he mentions the real actors in a nefarious business, which he was determined should be charged on William Penn.

The next allegation is, that William Penn was actuated by a strong attraction for exhibitions, which *humane* men generally avoid. The criminal code which the Legislator of Pennsylvania established in his colony, from which capital punishment was excluded, except for the crime of murder, might have caused a less prejudiced writer, to hesitate before charging Penn with a want of humanity. The occasion for this allegation, was the presence of William Penn, at the execution of two persons cruelly put to death, for having humanely afforded shelter to some of those engaged in the rebellion. The real motive which influenced him, has been given by Clarkson, on the authority of Bishop Burnett, who was no friend of Penn; it was to enable him to make a true report to the King, and the more efficiently to remonstrate with him against these vindictive punishments. Again, we are told, that the King desiring to win over the dissenters, nominated William Kiffin, an influential baptist, to be an alderman of London. This man, whose two grandsons had been executed for alleged complicity in the rebellion, regarded the existing government with abhorrence, and earnestly sought to avoid the proposed honor. Macaulay alleges, in his text, that William Penn, "was employed in the work of seduction, but to no purpose," and refers in a note to two authorities, one of which does not allude to Penn, and the other is the statement of Kiffin, that he had himself sought William Penn's influence to be excused from serving.

The manly course which Penn pursued in the case of the arbitrary proceeding of James, towards the fellows of Magdalen College, has been made the occasion by Macaulay of the grossest misrepresentation, and the most bitter reproach.

He affirms that the agency of Penn was employed "to terrify, caress, or bribe the fellows into submission;" he is said to have become "a broker in simony," and he is assumed without any adequate reason, and indeed, against all probability, to be the author of an anonymous letter, commencing with "Sir," and ending with "Your affectionate servant," while a contemporaneous entry on an official copy of the letter, expressly states, "Mr. Penn disowned this."

The facts are, that William Penn being at Oxford, when the King visited the place, found him greatly irritated, because the fellows had chosen Dr. Hough, President of the College, instead of the Bishop of Oxford, who was recommended by James, and was strongly suspected of Popery. He had threatened extreme violence, and justified the alarm which his language created by his subsequent acts. William Penn called on the fellows, hoping that some concession might be practicable; but when he heard their statements, he magnanimously wrote to the King on their behalf, stating, "that their case was hard," that "they could not yield without a breach of their oaths, and that such mandates [as the King's] were a force upon conscience." Some time after one of the fellows received an anonymous letter, which he thought fit to attribute to William Penn, and to him he addressed a reply. He acknowledged Penn's former kind interference *in behalf of the College*, and plead his well-known employment of time in doing good to mankind, and using his credit with the King for the benefit of those who might have been misrepresented to him, as reasons for asking his mediation with James. Whether William Penn replied to this letter, is not known; we only know that he disavowed the authorship of that which had occasioned it. Some time after, a deputation from the fellows visited William Penn at Windsor — an account of what passed, is extant in a letter from Dr. Hough, the newly-elected President. It is upon this paper that Macaulay founds his severest charges against Penn; and how shamefully he has tortured it to effect his purpose, the following statement, the result of an able examination of the document by the late Editor of the Tablet, will show:—

"Mr. Macaulay represents Penn as employed to

solicit the fellows; Dr. Hough represents the fellows as coming to solicit him.

"Mr. Macaulay says that, after many professions of friendship, Penn 'began to hint at a compromise;' Dr. Hough says, 'he did not so much as offer at any proposal by way of accommodation, which was the thing I most dreaded.'

"Mr. Macaulay makes his readers believe that the topics urged by Penn, were urged to persuade them to compromise; Dr. Hough describes them as used to convince the fellows that there was little hope of success from his intercession.

"Mr. Macaulay represents Penn as trying to overcome the scruples of the fellows to the commission of perjury; Dr. Hough represents him as admitting that the fellows gave satisfactory answers to his 'objections.'

"Mr. Macaulay represents Penn as talking the merest drivel, relying solely on James's moderation, and willing to give the 'Papists' two or three colleges in mere wanton injustice; Dr. Hough (most unwillingly) shows that Penn thought the 'Papists' had a right to two or three colleges, and believed they would abstain from further demands, because it would be dangerous to ask for more.

"Mr. Macaulay describes the result of the interview as the 'breaking off of a negotiation' by the fellows; Dr. Hough describes it as the concession of a favour by Penn.

"In short, in every part of it, in general and in detail, no version of the interview could be imagined or invented, more remote from the truth than that given by Mr. Macaulay. It is true, that when somebody mentioned the Bishop of Oxford's indisposition, Penn 'smiling,' asked the fellows how they would like Hough to be made a Bishop. This remark, made as a joke, answered by Mr. Cradock as a joke, and even by Dr. Hough, who answered it more seriously—not taken as an 'offer at any proposal by way of accommodation'—this casual piece of jocosity—picked out of a three hours' conversation—reported by one interlocutor without the privity of the other—and, if taken seriously, at variance with every other part of the conversation, and unconnected with its general tenor, is gravely brought forward as a proof that a man, otherwise honest, deliberately intended to use 'simony' as a bait to tempt a divine to what both parties *knew* to be 'perjury.'

"If Mr. Macaulay were Crown counsel, arguing for Penn's conviction before a common jury, such a 'point' would be too gross even for the license of the Old Bailey. But, if this be admitted as a canon, not of the venal advocate, but of the grave historian, who, by virtue of his function, is bound to judicial soberness and impartiality, what help is there for the characters of honest men.

"Surely, then, an examination into the true facts of this Oxford business, makes it not unjust to Mr. Macaulay to assert, that his charges against Penn of 'intimidation,' of being a 'broker in simony of a peculiarly discreditable kind,' of endeavours 'to tempt a divine to perjury,' to 'terrify or bribe' men to forsake 'the path of right,' are all groundless; that his statement, that even in the first instance he was employed by the Court, is unproved; and that the impression given, that he was its agent in the last and most important interview, is the very reverse of the truth; the requests for his intercession, which (says Forster) his reputation for 'doing good to mankind,' and honest struggles to 'undeceive' the King, induced such men as Bailey to make to him, being construed, as in the case of Kiffin, into attempts on his part to seduce and efforts to frighten.

"It would be hard to find any other history, in which the very virtues of a man are thus twisted into grounds for the most injurious attacks upon his character."

It has frequently been charged upon William Penn, and Macaulay renewed the allegation, that, in his "intemperate" zeal for religious liberty, he had supported the King in attempting to rule without the aid of Parliament. But there is positive evidence, well known to Macaulay, which proves that the reverse was the truth. "Penn," says Sir James Mackintosh, quoting contemporary authority, "desired a Parliament as the only mode of establishing toleration without subverting the laws;" and in the Yearly Meeting's Address to the King, on the occasion of his "Christian Declaration for liberty of conscience," which was presented by William Penn, it was expressly stated, that they looked "to such a concurrence from Parliament, as may secure it to their posterity in after times."

On a review of William Penn's whole conduct, in connection with King James, it is perfectly clear, that he abetted the Court in no act of cruelty or injustice, conspired with it in no effort to despoil the established Church of England, but used all his influence, and even plainly remonstrated with the King against such acts, and such efforts; that while he wrote and laboured assiduously for the promotion of civil and religious liberty, he earnestly advocated its establishment by authority of law, and not by an unconstitutional edict of the monarch. It is also clearly proven, that his modern traducer, while carefully selecting, and greatly misconstruing, such passages as might in this way be made to injure Penn's character, has as carefully declined to notice others which clearly establish his innocence, even when quoting such authorities for other purposes.

It remains to notice those statements which have reference to the alleged efforts of William Penn to replace James on the throne of England. Our review of the absurd charges which Macaulay has reproduced under this head, will be brief. If true, they involve a total abnegation by Penn, of principles, to the promotion of which he had given himself from his youth, for which he had suffered the severance of the closest family ties, had undergone severe imprisonment, had sacrificed his fortune, and had perilled his life. Had clear historical evidence substantiated these charges, we would have been, however reluctantly, obliged to confess that one of the noblest contributions to the cause of morals, of liberty and religion, which the world has yet witnessed, was made by a man, who, ere he had passed middle life, had basely abandoned the cause which he had espoused, and turned back again with singular avidity into the paths of folly and of vice. The world has yet to witness a more astounding fall from purity, and true nobility of character, to the grossest depravity combined with consummate hypocrisy, than that which is presented in the life of the Founder of Pennsylvania, if Macaulay be a truthful historian. Happily for the cause of truth, virtue, and human progress, their enemy is not Penn, but his assailant.

In his third and fourth volumes, Macaulay has charged William Penn with being one of a band of conspirators to restore King James, by the aid of the French army. On this charge Penn had been tried before the Privy Council, at a time when popular prejudice was against him, on account of his former intimacy with James, and acquitted. But this does not satisfy our scrupulous historian. He rests his allegation upon the confession of one of the conspirators. This man, Preston, we are told, named Penn as one of his associates in the plot; and, upon his evidence, warrants were issued against him. Happily, the historian most effectually discredits his only witness, when he tells us what sort of a person he was. It appears, from this statement, that he was convicted of treason, and under sentence of death; had witnessed the execution of a fellow conspirator, who refused to make a confession; was promised that his life should be spared, if he would make disclosures; that he was wholly unmanned by his situation; that the struggle between "pride, conscience, and party spirit," on the one side, and "intense love of life," on the other, was severe; that under the stimulus of wine, he was bold in refusing to confess, but weak and wavering, when the excitement was passed; that he "wrote a confession every forenoon when sober, and burned it every night when merry." "The fatal hour drew nigh, and the fortitude of Preston gave way." He made his pretended disclosures, was released, and retired to pass the rest of his life with "blighted fame, and a broken heart." If it were needful to disprove the evidence given under such circumstances, by a witness so utterly discredited by the historian himself, it would be quite sufficient to revert to the subsequent acquittal of Penn after trial, and to the remarkable fact, that not one of the parties named by Preston suffered further inconvenience from his allegations against them, than restraint so brief, as clearly to show, that the government placed no reliance upon the testimony of the witness.

When examined at his own request before the Privy Council on this charge, William Penn declared himself a faithful subject to William and Mary, protesting, as in the Divine presence, that he knew no plot, unless the projects of the French government might be such. With a levity not unworthy of the folly of his assertion, Macaulay calls this telling something very like a lie, "and confirming it by something very like an oath." Having completely discredited his only authority for a statement at variance with Penn's honest declaration, the historian's charge of falsehood needs no further refutation, while a reverent affirmation of the truth, as in the Divine presence, was, as is well known, not esteemed by W. Penn, or his contemporaries, to partake of the character of an oath.

There are few things more remarkable than the fact, that when Macaulay brings a serious charge against William Penn, he almost invariably relies upon authority, the value of which he himself elsewhere utterly destroys. In his fourth volume, he gravely tells, that no sooner had William Penn been acquitted of the charges brought against him, than he sent a message to King James, earnestly exhorting him to invade England with 30,000 men. For this assertion, he gives two authorities: one is a paper drawn up at St. Germains, under the direction of Melfort; the other is Avaux, the representative of the French King in the camp of James, when he invaded Ireland. Statements so difficult of belief, would seem to require at least one responsible witness, and a severe examination. Taking his own estimate of his authorities for these grave charges, we are forced to the conclusion, that they have been made without the testimony of a single credible witness, and with inconceivable recklessness.

Melfort, he tells us, "was an apostate, he was believed to be an insincere apostate;" again, Melfort, it is said, "was a renegade, he was a mortal enemy of his country; he was of a bad and tyrannical nature;" "the abhorrence of England and Scotland." Speaking of some intercepted letters, he says, "they proved to be from Melfort, and were worthy of him — every line indicated those qualities which made him the abhorrence of his country;" and, in another place, he charges him with "a certain audacious baseness which no English statesman could emulate." If we test the value of the evidence borne by Avaux, it is equally worthless.

There is some question whether the statement of the man warrants the conclusions drawn from it. But, if it does, inasmuch as William Penn had a few months before declared, that "he never had the wickedness to think of endeavouring to restore" James to the throne of England, it is simply a question of veracity between Penn and Avaux, endorsed by Macaulay. But, the latter has but a few pages before, given us his opinion of his own witness. "It is not too much to say that, of the difference between right and wrong, Avaux had no more notion than a brute; one sentiment was to him in the place of religion and morality, a superstitious and intolerant devotion to the crown which he served. This sentiment pervades all his despatches, and gives a colour to all his thoughts and words." In a question, then, of truthfulness, between William Penn and the Count of Avaux, few will probably hesitate. But, it is more difficult to determine the precise position on the scale of morals of that writer, who dares to pollute the stream of history with the feculence of one, whom he had himself ranked in moral sensibility with the brutes.

We cannot better conclude this little volume, than by inserting the following eloquent and instructive passages from the pamphlet, which has supplied the larger portion of the material for this chapter.*

Speaking of William Penn, the writer remarks, "he was not a man who could make one duty an excuse for shirking another: within his conscience there was no conflict between the claims of religion and patriotism: he did not fly from the world, but faced it with true words and true deeds, as one who, as he said himself when, during the storm of persecution, he rebuked a powerful persecutor, 'was above the fear of man, whose breath is in his nostrils, and must one day come to judgment, because he only feared the living God, that made the heavens and the earth.' This reverential fear of God — this it was that made him fearless of man, that gave him 'integrity' to 'stand firm against obloquy and persecution,' and not against them alone, but gave him power over himself; strength to resist temptations from within as well as to sustain violence from without; for it must be borne in mind, that he was not one of those who take to piety only when wearied of pleasure, ceasing to pluck the rose because they have been pricked by its thorns. This 'strong sense of

---

* William Penn and Thomas B. Macaulay. — By W. E. Forster.

religious duty' was not his because his other senses were weak, or because he had satiated them; nor did he refrain from enlisting himself in the service of God till he had proved Mammon to be a hard master, but, in the strength of his passions, he controlled them: in the spring-time of life, when the prizes of pleasure and ambition were before him, he chose the path of self-denial, and walked in it to the end.

"And, this son of a courtier, who thus preferred a prison to a court; who chose as the companions of his youth, men, whose very name was a bye-word of scorn, who, until his forty-first year, had led a life of consistent self-control, and proved his sincerity by his sufferings and sacrifices, can it be believed that he could have thus suddenly found his 'resolution give way,' even though 'courtly smiles and female blandishments, had been 'offered' as 'bribes to his vanity?' "

Mr. Macaulay's faith in human virtue must indeed have been sorely tried—his estimate of the strength of religious duty must be but slight—or, instead of suspecting "the eminent virtues of such a man," he would have questioned the probability of so strange a fall. But, like most men who are over-doubting in one direction, he is too believing in another, for, if he has little faith in the truth of Penn's professions, he has at least a firm confidence in the certainty of his own suspicions — if he be sceptical of virtue, he compensates for it by being credulous of vice; and so, if he refuses to listen to the concurrent testimony of "rival nations and hostile sects," he yet gives full credence to the insinuations of party prejudice, and makes up for his disbelief in the general estimate of Penn's character by an admission of charges, respecting which it is hard to discover the facts of which they are the distortion.

But the voice of history cannot be thus silenced: she has already recorded her judgment, from which there is no appeal; nor should Mr. Macaulay cavil at its justice, for, strange as it may seem to him, there is in it no mystery.

This Quaker was a strong and a brave, and therefore a free man: he ruled himself, and fearing God, feared no other; and so he made posterity his debtor, for, that spirit which won freedom for himself, he left to it as a legacy, and there is no fear that the debt due to him will be unpaid, so long as the inheritance remains.

The memory of good men is sacred: we treasure it, as we value our safety in the present — our hope for the future; for, on what, after all, depends our national freedom, of which Mr. Macaulay so often and so loudly vaunts? — most assuredly not, as he would seem to think,* on the limitations of the prerogative of our rulers, handed down to us from our ancestors, but on that spirit of individual justice, which, inasmuch as it breathed in their hearts, made that freedom both possible and necessary, of the

---

* Macaulay, vol. i. chap. 1.

strength whereof these limitations were and are the exact measure. It is not to the fact that for ages past Englishmen have had the habit of preventing their kings from taking their money, or making or breaking laws at their pleasure, that they owe what liberties they possess. These "three great constitutional principles," * as Mr. Macaulay calls them, are indeed the signs of our freedom, their prevalence has been the measure of its growth, but to suppose them to be its origin is to commit the absurdity of taking the effect for the cause. Individual self-government, that alone is the cause of national freedom — the source and guarantee of the liberty of the subject — for that alone makes personal liberty compatible with social order; and of this power of self-control, the force whereof gauges the freedom of all governments, and without which all constitutions — yes, even the "glorious constitution of 1688" — are mere waste-paper—of this power the highest possible ideal is "a strong sense of religious duty."

Alas, then, for our liberties, if ever, as a nation, we follow the example of Mr. Macaulay, and reverence, in place of this spirit, those forms which are but its expression, for then indeed will they become to us a mockery and a stumbling-block, but until we do so, there is no fear that we shall forget that "for the authority of law, for the security of property, for the peace of our streets, for the happiness of our

* Macaulay, vol. i. p. 29.

homes, our gratitude is due," not alone ' to the Long Parliament, to the Convention, and to William of Orange," *—to them indeed, but if to them, then also to that "mythical person," whose life, grotesque as may have been its garb, was, more than that of any politician of his day, the incarnation of this spirit of self-control, and whose words and deeds yet dwell within our memories as witnesses of its power.

---

* Macaulay, concluding paragraph of vol. ii.

# APPENDIX.

(See page 81.)

A REMARKABLE confirmation of the truth of this testimony in favour of the Indians, is found in the speech of Senator Houston of Texas, during the debate on the Army bill in the United States Senate, in the session of 1857–8. He said: —

"I was associated with the Indians, for they were in the army of Jackson in the Creek Nation. After that, in 1817, when still a subaltern in the army, I was appointed an agent by the government — the first sub-agent that ever was appointed: and for twelve months I was again associated with them in the transaction of business, and renewed the old associations of boyhood. After the duties of my agency were over, occasionally those associations were preserved, and when, in after life, reverses came upon me, and dark clouds fell upon my pathway, I spent in exile four years with the Indians, with various tribes. Tell me I do not understand the Indian? Too well I understand his wrongs. Tell me that, with all the advantages of education, and all the bright associations of the world, and in all the galas of fashion, you are to learn the Indian's character and disposition, and the history of his wrongs! No, sir, they are in tradition: they are not in history, and I have learned them. I know them. I know his disposition;

I know it well, and better than any officer who is on the frontier of the United States.

If I had not the experience which I have cited, this might be considered boasting; but I feel that I only state the truth. I know that their character is as I have stated, for I have not failed to conciliate them wherever I have tried; and how? By even-handed justice. Hold the scales of justice suspended with a steady hand between yourself and the Indian, and you will have no danger from him: it will not be necessary to suspend the sword above his head, like the sword of Damocles. Why, sir, with one twentieth part of the money expended to support the army, or even less, you could feed the Indians on our borders, and clothe them in comfortable garments; and then you would need no army except to take care of your fortresses, and keep your arms in order; for I am sure you never can rely on a regular army, unless you make it like the European armies, of hundreds of thousands of men."

THE END.

www.ingramcontent.com/pod-product-compliance
Lightning Source LLC
LaVergne TN
LVHW011236110826
845150LV00006B/1656

* 9 7 8 1 4 2 5 5 1 4 2 2 8 *